Anna Pavlova
Genius of the Dance

Ellen Levine

SCHOLASTIC
HARDCOVER

Scholastic Inc. New York

Copyright © 1995 by Ellen Levine.

All rights reserved. Published by Scholastic Inc.
SCHOLASTIC HARDCOVER is a
registered trademark of
Scholastic Inc.

No part of this publication may be reproduced in whole or in part,
or stored in a retrieval system, or transmitted in any form or by any
means, electronic, mechanical, photocopying, recording, or other-
wise, without written permission of the publisher. For information
regarding permission, write to Scholastic Inc.,
555 Broadway, New York, NY 10012.

Library of Congress Cataloging-in-Publication Data
Levine, Ellen.
Anna Pavlova, genius of the dance / by Ellen Levine.
p.   cm.
Includes bibliographical references (p. 144) and index.
ISBN 0-590-44304-6
1. Pavlova, Anna, 1881–1931 — Juvenile literature. 2. Ballet
dancers — Soviet Union — Biography — Juvenile literature.
[1. Pavlova, Anna, 1881–1931. 2. Ballet dancers.]   I. Title.
GV1785.P3L48   1995
792.8'028'092 — dc20

[B]   94-7310
                                                         CIP
                                                          AG

12 11 10 9 8 7 6 5 4 3 2 1   5 6 7 8 9/9 0/0

Designed by Elizabeth B. Parisi
Printed in the U.S.A.   37
First printing, March 1995

For Lenore Kodner Israel,
who first took me to the ballet
and inspired me to love it.

Contents

Acknowledgments

I am most grateful to Karen Backstein for suggesting that I write the story of Pavlova. Because of her deep commitment to books about dance for young people, I have had the wonderful experience of "living intimately" with the extraordinarily creative and passionate spirit of Anna Pavlova.

I am beholden to Tim Peck for his most careful reading of the manuscript and his fine and thoughtful editing.

I am also grateful to Anton Chekhov. Whenever I have felt daunted by the task of writing about Pavlova, I have found comfort in his words: "I don't understand anything about the ballet; all I know is that during the intervals the ballerinas stink like horses."

Author's Note

Pavlova spoke English with a Russian accent, and her spoken English was not always grammatically correct. Some who knew her and wrote of their personal experiences with her quoted Pavlova as speaking in broken English. Others, to convey the fluency of her thought, if not her words, quoted her without any suggestion of an accent. I have kept all the quoted material as it originally was written. The short autobiographical notes Pavlova wrote were no doubt translated from Russian or French, for she was fluent in both.

Preface

Before Anna Pavlova left her home in Russia in 1910 and traveled abroad, scarcely anyone in the United States had seen a ballet performance. And that was also true for much of the world outside of western Europe and Russia.

Pavlova believed that every person can be moved by art, by beauty. She felt it her mission to bring ballet to as many people as she could. She traveled from England to China, Russia to America, Australia to South Africa. She danced for anyone who would come to a performance — peasants and kings, children and adults. She appeared before more audiences than any other performer of her time.

During her life, she was considered the world's greatest ballerina. It was not for her technical skill. Great though it was, there have been more technically perfect dancers. But Pavlova touched people. She could make an audience smile or cry, or gasp at a fleeting moment of beauty. She was a maker of dreams.

Anna at age nine, presumably with her mother.

On a Cold Winter Day

On a cold winter day at the end of January, 1881, in St. Petersburg, Russia, a baby girl was born to a laundress named Lyubov Feodorovna. The little one was two months early, and no one was certain how long she would live. She was christened on Saint Anna's Day on the Russian Orthodox Church calendar. And so she was called Anna.

Little Anna was kept wrapped in wool for the first months of her life and put in the care of her grandmother in the country village of Ligovo. Everyone thought the clean air fifty miles away from St. Petersburg would be better than the congestion of the city. Little Anna, although she remained thin, grew stronger.

Anna never lived with her real father. When the child was very young, her mother married Matvey Pavlov, a peasant and reserve soldier in the Tsar's army. As an adult Anna always said her father died when she was two years old. She must have meant Matvey Pavlov, for he was the only father she had ever known. From that age on, Anna lived alone with her mother and in the summers with her grandmother as well.

Anna and her mother were quite poor. Some days the only food they had to eat was rye bread and cabbage soup. But Anna did not feel deprived. Although her mother worked hard, she made special treats for Anna whenever she could.

In St. Petersburg they lived in a tiny, cozy apartment. Her mother was a devout believer in the Russian Orthodox religion, and in the living room a candle was lit in front of an *icon* of the Virgin Mary. As a young girl, Anna used to tell the picture all her hopes and dreams. She felt that the Virgin's kind eyes were looking deeply into her own, and that the Virgin understood all that was inside her.

Anna loved the summers at her grandmother's *dacha*, the little cottage in Ligovo. Departure day for the country was hectic and exciting. Her mother would hire a wagon on which they would pile their bedding, *samovar*, pots, skillets, dishes, clothing, and the icon. They always brought as much furniture as they could, since her grandmother was also very poor and had few things.

The village of Ligovo was surrounded by fields and woods owned by wealthy landowners. Anna spent a great deal of time in these woods playing by herself in the patches of wildflowers. She loved to find the earliest snowdrops in the spring. She played where the lilies of the valley grew freely, and in the late summer and fall she picked berries and wild mushrooms. All her life, she was to love the dark fir trees and the swaying birches of the Russian forests.

A Magic Night

It was Christmas. The little fir tree in Anna's apartment in St. Petersburg was decorated with gold-painted fruits that glowed as they turned in the soft candlelight.

Tonight, however, Anna wasn't watching the shining fruit. She peered intently out the window. Snow was falling, big flakes, wet and sticky. Eagerly she waited for the carriage-sleigh that would take her and her mother to the Maryinsky Theater. Anna was going to see her first ballet performance, *The Sleeping Beauty*.

"You are going to enter fairyland," her mother said as their sleigh sped through the dark streets. Just as Anna was beginning to despair that they'd never arrive, the sleigh pulled up alongside many others at the theater doors. Light streamed onto the street. Sleigh doors flew open as hundreds of people rushed from the cold night air into the warm theater. The horses stomped their hooves and snorted as they shifted to keep warm.

Almost everyone was wearing stylish cloaks,

elegant hats, and jeweled gloves. In all her life, Anna had never seen such a parade of wonders. She and her mother took their seats, and as the orchestra began tuning their instruments, Anna shivered slightly. The lights dimmed, and people shifted expectantly. In the darkness, the curtain slowly rose to the opening chords of the music.

On stage was a great palace hall filled with royal visitors for the christening of the baby princess Aurora. Without words, the dancers told the story of *The Sleeping Beauty*, a story eight-year-old Anna knew by heart. She sat entranced as each of the fairy godmothers whirled, dipped, and glided across the stage.

Anna hardly knew what to look at first. Costumes, fantastic in design and color . . . scenery, awesome in its grandeur . . . musicians, filling the cavernous theater with beautiful sounds. And most of all, the dancers. She sighed with pleasure as each of the fairy godmothers offered special gifts for the Princess.

All at once the music seemed to darken, and a terrible roar filled the palace hall. Anna shrank back in her seat as the evil Fairy Carabosse, with her dreadful rat attendants, swept in. Carabosse grinned wickedly as she leaned toward the Princess. Suddenly the Lilac Fairy godmother danced forward. "Yes, she will prick her finger," she seemed to be saying as she crossed the stage, "but no, she will not die, only sleep till awakened by a prince's kiss!"

Anna held her breath, afraid to move, wrapped in the spell of this enchantment. As the second act began, she leaned forward to watch a crowd of young men and women dance a beautiful waltz.

"Niura," her mother whispered Anna's nickname, "would you like to dance like that?"

"Oh no!" Anna said quickly. "I want to dance like the beautiful woman who is the Princess. I want to be Aurora!"

Her mother smiled, never suspecting for a moment that one day Anna would be Princess Aurora, the Sleeping Beauty.

All the way home, Anna was silent. She knew she had to dance, just as she had to breathe. She knew she would dance, and she knew that dance would be her life.

That night she dreamed she was moving as freely and lightly as a butterfly in summer.

Too Young

The next morning Anna begged her mother, "Dear Mamasha, you'll let me learn to dance — you want me to, don't you?"

"Why yes, Niura, yes, of course," her mother answered absentmindedly.

How could a young child be so intent on something? She'll get over it, Anna's mother thought. But Anna was persistent. She talked of nothing else. She begged, she cried, she pleaded.

At last her mother said, "In order to become a dancer, you would have to leave me and go to the Ballet School." She paused. "My little Niura doesn't want to leave me — I'm sure of that!"

"No," Anna answered solemnly. "But if I must in order to become a dancer, then I will." Anna hugged her mother and again begged to be taken to the Ballet School.

At last her mother agreed and arranged for an interview with the principal. Anna barely slept the two nights before the great event.

On the day of the interview, Anna and her mother walked past the Alexandrinsky Theater, along the smooth cobblestoned street, until they reached an enormous yellow building with tall marble columns. The school was inside.

The Ballet School, part of the Imperial theater system, was founded by the Tsars in 1735, nearly a hundred and fifty years before Anna was born. The school was rich in tradition. Its goal was to produce dancers excellent enough to perform on the stage of the great Maryinsky Theater, the theater at which Anna had seen the production of *The Sleeping Beauty*.

When Anna and her mother passed through the massive wooden doors of the school, they were directed to the administration office. Anna stood trembling in front of a bearded man who had the power to say "Yes" or "No." He looked closely at her. "The regulations forbid us to take a child of eight," he said to Lyubov Feodorovna. "Bring her again when she reaches her tenth birthday." Anna was devastated.

The winters passed slowly. At last it was the second spring and then summer. During that long waiting summer, Anna roamed the Ligovo woods, playing with flowers and animals, and dancing for hours the ballets of her dreams.

The house at Ligovo had many mice. Too many, her mother and grandmother thought. The two women set traps, but oddly, the mice didn't go after the bait. It was a while before Anna's mother discovered that Anna was secretly feeding the mice. Over the years, this family story was told many times. "And so you see, little Niura truly loves animals," the storyteller always ended.

One warm summer day, Anna was playing in an open grassy field. The air was still, and the butterflies floated lazily while Anna danced a scene from *The Sleeping Beauty* ballet. A young boy from the village wandered by. He reached up, caught one of the butterflies, and before Anna even realized what he was doing, he crushed it to death.

Anna never forgot that moment when the boy so easily and so senselessly killed a living thing. In later years, she confided to her husband that the killing of the butterfly was the first tragedy of her life. "It was," Anna said, "as if some giant had reached up his hand and pulled down the sky."

When the summer was over, Anna and her mother returned to their apartment in St. Petersburg. Lyubov Feodorovna unpacked all their belongings.

The fall was beginning. It was time to go back to the Ballet School.

The First Dance Class

Girls and boys gathered in the main hall of the Ballet School for the entrance examinations. Soon they were ushered up a flight of stairs into a large room where portraits of the Imperial family hung on the walls. Anna stared at the pictures. They seemed so lifelike. Could they tell how much she wanted to dance?

The directors of the school lined up the children in pairs and marched them into an adjoining room. Examiners sat at tables at one end of the room. All the children sat on benches. There were many girls from rich families, who wore beautiful clothes. Anna was afraid the examiners would never notice her.

One by one each child was called to the front table and told to walk the length of the room and then to run. The examiners looked to see if the child moved gracefully or awkwardly. Everyone's legs, especially the knees, were peered at and poked. Notes were carefully made.

Some children were dismissed after this first review. The remaining applicants were taken to the infirmary, where they undressed. A doctor listened carefully to each one's heartbeat, felt the spine, and checked everyone's eyesight and hearing. When the doctor was finished, all the children were given tea and lunch.

After the break, the examinations continued in the music room. A teacher played a scale, and each child had a turn at singing the notes. Then everyone was tested in reading, writing, and arithmetic.

At last the children assembled to hear the final results. The names of those who were accepted as students were read slowly and distinctly. Anna waited, half listening,. half praying. Then she heard her name — Anna! She was to be a student after all.

At the school, the administrators took complete charge of the students' lives, providing food, clothing, shoes, books, medical care, and anything else each student might need. Everything was free of charge, whether you came from a rich family or a poor one. This was particularly wonderful for Anna, whose mother earned very little money.

The daily schedule at the school rarely changed. Every morning at eight o'clock, a great bell awakened the students, and they quickly washed and dressed. First-year girls wore brown dresses. If they passed a very strict examination at the end of the school year, they were permitted to continue as students. Then they wore blue dresses with full skirts and white or black aprons, white stockings, and black shoes.

Every morning the students washed in cold water. But Friday was hot-bath day. The girls walked to a separate building and undressed in the bathhouse dressing room. Red-hot stones were piled high in a large stove, and maids poured water on the stones, creating a room full of steam. The girls scrubbed themselves and washed their hair. Hot-bath day was a welcome break from the daily routine.

When all the girls had finished washing and dressing, a teacher checked to see that their nails were clean and everyone's hair was neatly combed. Then the students went to pray in the little school chapel. One child would read the prayers aloud, standing in front of a flickering icon light that was always kept lit. At nine o'clock, everyone had morning tea, bread and butter.

After chapel and tea, the first dance classes began. The students assembled in a large, bright room with benches along the walls, a piano, and enormous mirrors that went from floor to ceiling. Portraits of the Russian Imperial family lined the walls. Anna's favorite was the picture of Empress Catherine II, whose "laughing eyes," Anna once told a friend, "seemed to look straight at us, as if following each *pas*, criticizing and encouraging us."

In addition to classical ballet, the students learned Russian folk dances and the national dances of many countries — Poland, Hungary, Spain, Italy, India, and others. Ballroom dancing and pantomime were also part of their instruction. Boys were taught certain leaps, and how to hold and support the girl dancers. Girls and boys studied separately, except for ballroom dancing classes.

At noon the students ate lunch and went outside for a fifteen- to twenty-minute stroll around a small garden in the courtyard. Warm or cold, wet or sunny, the school regimen called for a daily walk outdoors. Classes then continued until four o'clock in the afternoon. Unlike the morning dance classes, in the afternoon pupils studied mathematics, history, geography, science, and languages. After dinner and a short rest, there were fencing lessons, music classes, and special training in applying stage makeup.

One day on the weekend, parents were allowed to visit with their children. Anna's mother usually came every other week, since she had such a heavy work schedule.

Most days the students had supper at eight P.M., and an hour later, they were in bed.

The Tsar Is Coming!

Two by two, always in twos, the students marched to each meal. Their teachers counted them as they walked by. But it hadn't always been that way. Years past — no one remembered exactly how many — there had been a student at the school called "Lunatic Ann." She was very beautiful, but very nervous. To help calm her, Ann had special permission to practice the piano alone in the music room in the afternoons. She spent hours playing music and looking out the windows.

Ann fell in love with an officer of the Tsar's Horse Guards. When the young man drove his horses up and down Theater Street in the afternoon, Ann signaled to him from an upstairs window. Somehow, they arranged to meet.

One day Ann dressed up in a maid's uniform and covered her head with a shawl. She slipped through the pantry, down the back stairs, and out a side door to the street. She met her young officer and went off with him, never to be seen again. Several hours passed before anyone noticed she was missing, and it was years before anyone knew what had happened to Lunatic Ann.

One day when workmen were remodeling the students' closets, they noticed writing on the inside wall of one of the wardrobes. It had been Lunatic Ann's closet, and on the wall she had written out the whole story of her romance and planned elopement with the young officer. The escape plan had been there for anyone to see.

Since that time, the upstairs clear-glass windows had been replaced with frosted glass, and the girls were always lined up in twos and counted.

"Attention, girls! His Imperial Majesty Tsar Alexander III and Empress Marie are coming to watch a dance class," the teacher announced as Anna and her young classmates marched in twos on their way to the classroom. Everyone buzzed with excitement. Grand Duke Vladimir, the Tsar's brother, and other members of the Imperial family were also expected to attend.

The Ballet School was maintained by the Tsar's Court, and the Tsar frequently visited the school to watch special performances. Sometimes the Imperial family had tea in the school dining room. On those occasions the Tsar, also called the Emperor, and the Empress were very kind to the students. Anna and the others thought of them as a royal father and mother.

But the Imperial family had never watched Anna's class.

"What will happen if anyone makes a mistake?" the girls whispered among themselves.

The Tsar put the students at ease after the class, talking with all of them. He picked up Anna's close friend, Stanislava, and seated her on his knee. Suddenly Anna burst into tears, crying uncontrollably. The Tsar, puzzled, asked Anna what was the matter.

"Majesty, won't you take me as well as Stanislava?" she sobbed.

Quickly the Grand Duke reached out to comfort her. But she wept even louder, saying that she did not want a substitute for His Imperial Majesty!

The school director stood rigid with fear. Would the Tsar punish him for this foolish student's outburst? The other girls huddled anxiously in a group. No one said a word. The only sound was Anna's crying.

Suddenly the Grand Duke roared with laughter. "Oh, your Majesty!" he cried. "Oh, saints preserve us, but at last I am allotted my place. You are truly loyal, little one!" he said, smiling at Anna. The Tsar and his party had tea with the students, easing the awkwardness of the moment.

The Tsar Is Coming!

Many of the crowned heads of Europe knew of this incident, for over the years the Grand Duke told and retold the story many times, always laughing about it at his own expense.

Anna never made a scene like that again.

A Beautiful Line

Cod-liver oil! Anna thought it tasted awful.

Anna was a talented and hardworking student, but she had been a slender child, and remained that way as a teenager. Some said she looked a little like Marie Taglioni, the famous Italian ballerina who had retired from the stage many years before Anna was born. By the time Anna was a student, many of the famous ballerinas were stocky, some even a little plump. The school directors decided Anna needed to be fattened up a bit. And so the order came down — cod-liver oil.

Marie Taglioni was Anna's great idol, and Anna deeply regretted that she had never seen Taglioni perform. Taglioni was one of the first ballerinas to dance on *pointe,* on her toes. She was so graceful, so beautiful to watch, she seemed to float on air. The story is told that a highwayman once stopped her coach, stole nothing, but ordered her to dance for him.

In 1837, fifty-four years before Anna was a student at the Ballet School, Taglioni had traveled to St. Petersburg to dance in the Imperial Theaters for Tsar Nicholas I. She had rehearsed at the school before the first performance. The pupils, awed by the presence of such a famous dancer, had crowded around her. Up close she was a little woman with a wrinkled face. A few commented in Russian that she was a "funny little thing." One even rudely murmured, "Oh, what a freak you are."

But Marie Taglioni neither spoke nor understood Russian. She thought the students were complimenting her, and she politely said, "Thank you" in French. When the students later saw her dance, they were ashamed. She was beautiful to watch, light and elegant. She danced in what was called the *Romantic* style. Her ballet skirt was soft, and it folded and moved gracefully as she glided across the stage. In an outpouring of gratitude for her performance, for the first time in the history of the Maryinsky Theater, the audience threw flowers on the stage.

Anna Pavlova learned everything she could about Marie Taglioni, for to her Taglioni was ballet at its most perfect. But, like fashions in clothes, fashions in the styles of dancing change. When Anna was a student some fifty years after Taglioni had retired, the leading ballerinas danced in a different, less Romantic way. They often performed difficult technical, almost acrobatic, feats.

Pierina Legnani was one of the new Italian prima ballerinas. She danced in St. Petersburg when Anna was at the School. Legnani's special feat was to turn thirty-two *fouettés*, spins on one foot, one after another. The ballet students as well as the general theater audiences were fascinated by Legnani.

Because of Legnani, students practiced fouettés for weeks after. Christian Johanssen was a well-known and beloved teacher at the Ballet School. Johanssen opposed this Italian method of dancing, calling it acrobatic and belonging in a circus, not on an Imperial Theater stage. Enrico Cecchetti, another important teacher, had studied in Italy and was enthusiastic about the technical skills of the new dancers.

Above all the teachers was the ballet master and head of the Imperial Ballet Company, Marius Petipa. Though a Frenchman, he had danced, taught, choreographed, and directed at the Russian Imperial Theaters since the mid-1800s. Petipa walked a middle line between Johanssen and Cecchetti. After Legnani's performances, he allowed the Ballet School to hold some classes in the Italian method of dancing.

Anna worked hard at the technical feats, and like most of the students, she often practiced during her free time. But one of her teachers, Pavel Gerdt, was concerned about her strength. He

Bravi! Bravi!

The geography lesson had just started when the classroom door opened. The teacher who entered had a list in her hand, and Anna and the other students waited expectantly. Would the teacher announce there was to be a performance at the theater with a number of small roles for students? The magic word they all listened for was "rehearsal." Anna loved rehearsals. It was a chance to watch the professionals at work, and of course rehearsals meant the students missed afternoon classes.

The student dancers performed at the three large Imperial Theaters in St. Petersburg open to the public. Most often they danced in a ballet production. But sometimes they performed a dance sequence in an opera or drama. They went whenever and wherever they were needed. And in order to perform, of course they had to rehearse.

Rehearsing and dancing with the Imperial Company gave the students experience before paying audiences they could never get in a class-

thought she might harm herself attempting to copy Legnani.

Gerdt told Anna that her technique would develop over time. She had strong hips and thighs, but her legs were fine-boned, and her back, though flexible, was not that strong. She had the ability, he said, to move and stand in such a way that her whole body formed a beautiful line from the tips of her fingers down to her toes. Line was something that dancers talked and thought about. They worked hard to achieve a good line. Anna listened to Pavel and stopped trying to imitate Legnani.

room. A dancer always faces a physical risk, a danger. Will you slip and fall? Will your partner be in place to catch you when you leap through the air? Will you land properly when you jump and turn? How will you react if something unexpected happens to you?

In some ballets, large crowds of people had to be on stage, and children often played a part in these scenes. Sometimes they were pages to a King and Queen in a court scene. At other times they might dance the parts of flowers or animals. The audiences at the Imperial Theaters were accustomed to grand spectacles with fancy costumes of lace, velvet, frills, ruffles, and many jewels. Dressing up and putting on stage makeup was almost as much fun as performing.

The ballet Anna's teacher announced was *Paquita*. It was the students' favorite. In the last act, sixteen couples, thirty-two young people, performed a Polish dance called a *mazurka*. The audience always shouted *"Bravi! Bravi!"* when the students did this dance. Anna and her classmates thought it was a thrilling taste of what it might be like to be a professional ballet dancer.

The students whose names were called, and Anna was among them, left the geography class, gathered their practice clothes, and waited for the carriages that would take them to the theater. If they joined the ballet company after graduation

from school, carriages would bring them to the
theater for every performance and then take them
home after the show. In fact, each ballerina in
the company had her own private carriage, but
for now, six students rode together in one.

As a student, Anna appeared in an important
role at the Maryinsky Theater. The ballet was
called *Daughter of the Pharaoh*. Anna had spent
days rehearsing. On the evening of the performance, she carefully applied her makeup and was
helped into her costume. She was both excited
and nervous. She had seen dancers trip, and they
often strained muscles. But if it wasn't a serious
injury, you'd forget the pain while you danced.

Behind the curtain Anna silently made the sign
of the cross. Then, onstage in the center of the
lights, she felt wrapped in music and movement.
The notes . . . the rhythm . . . gliding to the sound
. . . it was all perfect! She danced smoothly toward the front of the stage. As she *pirouetted* and
stepped to the side, her foot banged against the
prompter's box on the floor of the stage. She fell
with her back to the audience.

Abruptly the theater became silent. What
would this young student do? Anna rose, smiled,
and then curtsied, as if asking everyone to forgive
her for her awkwardness. The audience, which
had gasped the moment she fell, now wildly applauded. After the performance was over, people

talked more about the charming Anna Pavlova than about the ballet itself.

The year after her "falling debut" at the Maryinsky Theater, Anna and her classmates graduated from the school. For their final examination, the students gave a dance performance at one of the theaters. Anna was in a ballet called *The Imaginary Dryads*. Her teacher, Pavel Gerdt, had choreographed a special section for her.

Although the public was allowed to attend the performance, a jury of the school staff and certain dance critics sat in the best seats. Based on the jurors' grading, students were invited to join the official Imperial Ballet Company.

In the audience that evening was Victor Dandré, a twenty-seven-year-old mining engineer and member of the St. Petersburg city council. He had brought his nephew, Michel, who at age fifteen already called himself a "balletomaniac." When Anna was onstage, Dandré told his nephew that this slender, graceful dancer was the one he liked most. Afterwards he said she was "full of expression . . . here was something individual, something that was not learnt by rote at school." She would be, he believed, "a future great artist." Although he didn't know it then, she would also be his future wife.

The jury agreed with Dandré that Anna was a most individual dancer and gave her very high marks. One of the critics said, "She at once caught the eyes of all."

After graduation, most students danced in the company's *corps de ballet*, but Anna was given the grade of first dancer, a *coryphée*. This meant she would have roles with two or three others instead of dancing with fifty or a hundred in the large corps. It was a promotion before she had even started to work, and Anna was thrilled.

Curtsy to the Right . . .
Curtsy to the Left . . .

It was called the "class of perfection," and Anna was a member. After graduation from the ballet school, the women and men dancers in the company continued to study in special classes. Just as a pianist practices scales, a dancer stretches, bends, turns, leaps, and repeats steps over and over again. Anna knew one dancer who felt he had to practice six hours a day. This made sense to her. She believed a real artist always works to improve, always tries new steps.

Anna studied with Christian Johanssen. In the class, she was often paired with another young dancer, Michel Fokine. She enjoyed working with him, for like her, he was devoted to the ballet.

Anna also went regularly to a class taught by Madame Sokolova, a former ballerina who had danced in most of the Imperial Company's ballets and was very familiar with the different roles. In Madame Sokolova's small studio, there was no room for a piano, and so Madame sang the music as she worked with dancers.

Anna and Madame Sokolova shared a passion for the theater. Madame used to say, "The stage before all," and that was how Anna felt. Anna danced because she loved to. She didn't think of it as a job, and she didn't think of it as providing a good salary, although both were true. For Anna, the ballet was a glorious form of art that was wonderful in itself.

Anna learned from Madame Sokolova that every part of the performance was equally important. After dancing a beautiful ballet, Sokolova thought it dreadful if a ballerina walked on flat feet to the front of the stage to take a bow. That, she announced fiercely, would totally destroy the mood of the performance. "Tripping lightly, you come into the middle, curtsy to the right — Imperial box; curtsy to the left — director; two steps forward . . . back now, raise your eyes, smile in curtsying to the gallery." And that's what Madame believed was correct. In later years, Anna's curtain calls were nearly as famous as her dances — they were little ballets in themselves.

Very early in her career, Anna began to receive favorable press reviews. After one evening's performance, a leading newspaper reviewer wrote,

Today there was a one-act ballet . . . in which . . . Mme Pavlova . . . graceful, ethereal, and elegant, danced delightfully. The ballet has made a fortunate acquisition in the person of this very young but unusually gifted dancer, who has come to the fore in such a short time.

Anna had been a member of the company for only four months when this was written!

The company master, Marius Petipa, recognized something special in Anna. Not long after she joined the company, Petipa placed her in the lead role in the ballet *The Awakening of Flora*, replacing his own daughter, who had danced for many more years than Anna.

The company had a long list of ballets in its repertoire that were frequently staged. Young dancers had many chances to play different parts. In her first season, Anna danced an important role in the famous ballet *Giselle*. She was deeply moved by this ballet, and in later years she danced the lead part of Giselle.

Anna also received public recognition for her role in another Petipa ballet, *Les Saisons* (*The Seasons*). This ballet was staged at the benefit performance of prima ballerina Mathilde Kchessinskaya. After twenty years with the Imperial Company, a leading ballerina would give a benefit performance, at which time she would be presented with lavish gifts and tributes. Kchessinskaya was given the special honor of a benefit after only ten years.

The ballet *The Seasons* is the story of the four seasons — cold Winter banished by Spring's flowers and birds, Summer's crops planted and growing, and a spectacular Fall finale danced by a God and Goddess of the Harvest, who had bunches of grapes and apples attached to their costumes and small cymbals strapped to their hands.

During the first section of the ballet, the *danseur* depicting Winter had four attendants: Frost, Ice, Hail, and Snow. Each had a solo dance, and Anna was Frost.

During a thirty-minute intermission at the benefit, attendants filled the entire stage with flowers. At the end of the evening, Kchessinskaya took many curtain calls. Then she turned to find the dancer whom the audience had enthusiastically applauded after the Frost solo. She brought Anna to the front of the stage for a special bow. This recognition by so famous a ballerina as Kchessinskaya was a sweeter tribute to Anna than any newspaper review. It was an honor from a colleague.

Paradise, Pavlovtzi, and Politics

The night of Kchessinskaya's benefit, Georg Kotschubei was in the audience. Georg had attended the opera and ballet since he was a child. He always sat in excellent seats that were reserved every year for his family.

The higher-priced seats, called the stalls, were not easy to get. They were jealously guarded, handed down from parents to children. The lovers of ballet in these families, the *balletomanes*, fiercely argued among themselves about their favorite dancers. If a favorite left St. Petersburg to travel a long day's train ride to Moscow for a performance, their fans often followed. When Kchessinskaya went to Moscow, the first row of orchestra seats at the Maryinsky Theater was empty the whole time she was gone. Her fans had followed her.

Those with less money, but as great a love for the ballet, sat in the gallery, upstairs. They were often young people, students, and they called the gallery "paradise" — perhaps because the seats were so high up. The Maryinsky Theater box office opened at eight o'clock in the morning for the sale of the gallery seats. On some nights, even in the depth of winter, people stood in a line that snaked around the theater, often waiting up to ten hours to buy tickets for a precious gallery seat. All her life Anna treasured the people who sat in the galleries in theaters all over the world, people with little money, but much love of art.

Georg Kotschubei, however, never had to wait in line. His father was a prince, with permanent box seats. Now, as a university student, Georg sat in his own seats with his friends. At the end of her benefit, Kchessinskaya brought Anna Pavlova to the footlights for a special bow. Georg told friends he saw Anna's "eyes lit with a feverish happiness."

Determined to meet this young dancer, Georg learned Anna's address and went to visit her in the tiny apartment she shared with her mother. They talked for hours of art and the ballet. Anna spoke of her idol, Marie Taglioni, and the Romantic tradition in ballet. They became good friends, and Georg introduced Anna to his circle. The young people went on carriage rides, picnics, and other outings. Georg had heard Anna's mother call her Niura, and so he and his friends all called her "little Niura." It was a happy time, a carefree time, for Anna.

Within a few years, Anna had a group of followers much larger than just Georg and his friends. These fans called themselves "Pavlovtzi," and they followed her career with great intensity. And Anna's career was proceeding rapidly. Within a few years she became a first soloist, then a ballerina, and finally a prima ballerina.

In the first years that Anna danced with the company, the two new directors of the Imperial Theaters hired artists never before connected with the theater to design costumes and sets. Léon Bakst and Alexandre Benois, two of the best known, created wildly colorful and exotic designs.

Sergei Diaghilev, a young law student who much preferred the arts to law, was hired to edit the Imperial Theaters' yearbooks. He also started a magazine called *The World of Art*, and formed a circle of young people enthusiastic about new possibilities for ballet, theater, and painting. Anna and her friend and dance partner, Michel Fokine, were part of this group.

The new directors made another very important change. They stopped inviting foreign ballerinas to be the lead dancers for a Maryinsky season. Anna and other young Russians had shown remarkable talent, and deserved, the directors believed, the chance to perform in the starring roles.

But change was happening not only in the world of the ballet. In 1904, the Japanese Navy attacked and defeated a Russian naval squadron. Soon the nation was caught up in a war effort. Tensions between different ethnic groups increased, and there was general discontent in the society at large. Groups of marauding peasants, often encouraged by local police and even church leaders, singled out their Jewish neighbors and beat and killed them in terrible riots called pogroms.

At the same time, other farmers, workers, and students demanded democratic reforms. They wanted certain liberties — freedom of speech, the right to meet in groups and talk about politics if they wished, equality for all people, and freedom of the press.

The Tsar, as the absolute ruler of the country, did not want to give up any of his powers. On a frigidly cold Sunday morning in late January, 1905, thousands of workers led by a priest peacefully marched to the Winter Palace. They had come, they said, to speak to "their Tsar." The Palace troops fired on the unarmed crowd, killing and wounding nearly a thousand people. This terrible massacre became known as "Bloody Sunday."

Anna was deeply moved by the strikes and horrified at the shootings. At a meeting of dancers after "Bloody Sunday," she gave a speech condemning the troops for firing on innocent people. "Workers," she insisted passionately, "are not the enemy!"

Strikes spread throughout the city. Factories, schools, and hospitals closed. It was a cold winter, and food and electric supplies were running low. People, frantic and fearful, gathered on street corners to listen to speeches.

A number of ballet company members, roused by the general turmoil, began to talk about reforms in their own profession. Anna and Fokine were among the leaders of a group that met almost every night at either her apartment or his. They drew up a petition of their grievances and a list of reforms. They demanded the right to choose their company manager, since they, and not the director of all the theaters, best understood their own needs. They wanted pay raises for certain categories of dancers whose salaries they felt were unjustly low, and they asked for a shorter work week. Very important to the dancers was their demand that the theater director rehire ballet master Marius Petipa, whom he had earlier fired. Anna was elected by the group to be one of the delegates to present the director with the petition of grievances and demands.

The theater director refused to meet with the delegates and instead exerted tremendous pressure on the dancers to give up their demands. The activists were accused of being disloyal to the Tsar, to the ballet company, and to the school that had trained them. The director posted lists in the theater offering the protesting dancers the chance to sign a paper renouncing their demands. There were hints that if they didn't sign, they might lose their jobs. Indeed there were even rumors that the whole company might be disbanded.

Anna refused to sign, but many of the dancers did sign the director's lists. One very popular member of the company, Sergei Legat, was so hounded that his will was broken, and at last he signed. Afterwards, despondent and in emotional turmoil over what he had done, he took his own life.

With the country nearly at a standstill, the Tsar agreed to some of the general demands for reform. He also approved an amnesty, a dropping of all charges against strikers and protesters. Although the Tsar's pronouncement was welcomed, it came too late for Sergei Legat. At his funeral, Anna rearranged all the flowers so that the large banner and wreath from the dancers was the most prominent. The inscription on the banner read,

Paradise, Pavlovtzi, and Politics

"To the first victim, at the dawn of the freedom of Art, from the newly united Ballet Company."

Anna, called a "nonconformist" by the theater management, was to cherish her whole life the idea of "freedom of Art."

Birth of the Swan

In the spring after the strikes had ended, the management of the Imperial Theaters announced in its official magazine, the *Journal of Orders*, that Anna Pavlova had been promoted to ballerina. Anna had risen quickly up the ranks of dancers. With each promotion there was a salary increase, and an increase as well in the supply of ballet slippers she was given. The theater provided shoes to its dancers that were handmade and shipped from Paris. Ballet shoes must be soft and flexible, but firm enough to support a dancer. They don't last long, and a dancer will wear out many pairs during a season.

A member of the Maryinsky corps de ballet was given a new pair of ballet shoes after every four performances. Anna, however, joined the company as a coryphée, one category above the corps, and so she received a new pair after every three performances. As a first soloist, she was given a new pair every night. And now as a ballerina, she had reached the high point — a new pair after each act.

Birth of the Swan

Anna was a hard worker. She would rehearse late into the night if necessary and practice on the Maryinsky stage whenever it was empty. One day she arrived for rehearsal and discovered that she had left her practice clothes at home. It was a long carriage ride from the theater back to her apartment. Rather than waste the time, Anna took off her street clothes, wrapped two towels around her, and worked for several hours, oblivious to the stunned stagehands who watched from the wings.

Even though she was a ballerina, Anna continued to take classes. With her salary increase, she and her mother moved to a larger apartment with enough space for a practice room. When retired ballet school master Enrico Cecchetti attended one of her performances in Moscow, she asked him his opinion of her work. He was very complimentary, but he also told her that she needed to strengthen her back. She persuaded him to move back to St. Petersburg so he could give her private lessons at her apartment. She studied this way with Cecchetti for two years.

During these early years, Anna's mother attended all of Anna's performances. In one ballet, Anna had to fall to the floor as if she were seriously hurt. Always an expressive dancer, Anna made the fall look frighteningly real. Her mother, seated in a gallery seat watching this ballet for the first time, cried out, "Anna, my Anna, my Anna!" and rushed backstage.

All this time Anna continued to be partnered by Michel Fokine. They were frequently paired in a *pas de deux*, a short dance for two people performed as part of a larger ballet. Fokine did high jumps, and Anna, pirouettes.

"Take it easy, we still have a great deal of music left," she whispered to him when he twirled her too quickly. "Hurry, hurry!" she said when they dragged a bit behind the conductor.

Fokine wasn't happy with the way the pas de deux seemed stuck into a larger ballet with no purpose of its own except to show the skills of the two dancers. He believed that since it had no real connection to the ballet, it took away from the ballet's meaning. He wanted to choreograph, to create his own ballets that would reflect his ideas about dance. The Maryinsky dancers often gave performances to raise money for different charities, and Fokine began to choreograph his own ballets for these performances.

Anna had become good friends with Victor Dandré, who had first seen her dance years earlier at her graduation. Dandré was on the board of directors of the Society for the Prevention of Cruelty to Children. When that charity needed to raise money, Anna suggested that Dandré ask Fokine to choreograph a ballet.

Fokine was delighted. He created a ballet called *Chopiniana*, to the music of Frédéric Chopin. Anna danced a beautiful waltz in a long white Taglioni-style skirt. Based on *Chopiniana*, Fokine later choreographed one of his most famous ballets, *Les Sylphides*. Years after, he said, "Had Pavlova not performed so marvelously, so delightfully, the Chopin waltz, I might never have created *Les Sylphides*."

When Fokine was asked to do a ballet for another charity performance, he decided to create one based on an Egyptian theme. One day as he was doing research at the museum, he found a picture of an Egyptian dance in which a snake was used. Fokine knew that Anna, who was to dance a leading role in this new ballet, had a special way with animals. He went to the zoo and arranged to borrow a snake for the dance.

Onstage Fokine lifted the snake over his head to show Anna what to do. Cold sweat ran down his forehead. He felt faint, but managed to finish the movement and hand the snake to Anna. Snakes weren't her favorite animals, but she danced as directed.

After the first performance of this ballet, called *Egyptian Nights*, the snake was returned to the zoo. It had curled around Anna's arm and gone to sleep, refusing to slither through her hands as Fokine had planned. After that, Anna danced with a prop made of oilcloth stuffed with cotton.

Fokine was always looking for new ideas for ballets. One day while driving in the countryside with Dandré, Dandré's nephew Michel, and Anna, they passed a small lake with a swan. Anna stopped the carriage and ran down to feed the swan the remains of their picnic lunch. Fokine pointed out to Michel the utter beauty of the scene — Anna in her white dress, bent over, her arm gracefully extended, reaching for the white swan. Not too long after, Fokine attended a concert reading of a poem called "The Dying Swan," the story of the last minutes in the life of the graceful bird. The image of Anna at the lake and the power of the poetry remained with him.

During the 1907 Maryinsky season, Anna agreed to appear in a charity performance for poor mothers and newborn babies, and she asked Fokine to create a dance for her. He was in his apartment playing the mandolin, practicing a section of Saint-Saëns' *Carnival of the Animals*, when she visited him.

"What about Saint-Saëns' *Swan*?" he asked. She thought that was perfect. They went back to her apartment, and Fokine danced in front of her while she was directly behind. Then Anna danced alone, and Fokine walked alongside, curving her arms and changing some poses as she moved.

Fokine wanted to combine classical technique with deep emotion.

"This dance aims," he said, "not so much at the eyes of the spectator, but at his soul, at his emotions." They worked quickly and intensely. In less than half an hour, they had created a gem of a ballet that itself lasted only a few minutes. It was called *The Dying Swan*.

The night of the charity performance, the audience watched an extraordinary event. As Anna danced, it almost seemed that her arms became wings. They fluttered, pulling her up to fly. Her head flung back, she danced on pointe, moving forward, sideways, back. Then swaying, then down, one leg bent under her body, the other extended. The swan tried to rise again. Its wings seemed to gather strength. But weakened, its life seeping away, it throbbed one last time, and then the swan moved no more.

A Real Princess

It was the summer of 1907 in Moscow, and Anna, Fokine, and a group of young Maryinsky dancers were performing there for several weeks. Fokine was the group's director. Free from the hovering theater management in St. Petersburg, he experimented in his choreography.

This was the first time Anna had performed away from home, and she discovered that she loved dancing before new audiences. Her idol, Marie Taglioni, had traveled extensively from her home in Italy to Paris, London, and even Russia. "Reading the story of Taglioni's life," Anna said, "gave me the idea of appearing in foreign countries."

Anna had also met and become friendly with Isadora Duncan, an American dancer who visited Russia in 1904 and again in 1907. Duncan rejected classical ballet, believing that traditional ballet positions and steps limited the artistic spirit. The Russians called her "Little Barefoot" because she danced without any shoes. As a tribute to Duncan, Fokine choreographed a ballet in her style of movement. The corps de ballet danced in make-believe bare feet, with toes painted on their tights.

Anna and Fokine and their circle of artist friends, including the brilliant designers Léon Bakst and Alexandre Benois, were excited by Duncan's innovations. They didn't agree, of course, that classical ballet was a reactionary, old-fashioned form, for they themselves were experimenting and creating within ballet. But they shared with her a love of movement. During dinner at Anna's apartment, they all talked for hours about dance and art and beauty. Like Taglioni, Duncan had taken her ideas abroad.

For Anna the chance to see the world, share her art, learn what others were doing, was most appealing. After the Moscow trip, she began a tour of northern Europe. With Adolph Bolm as her partner, and a small group of Maryinsky dancers, Anna performed in Stockholm, Copenhagen, Prague, and Berlin.

The troupe was received enthusiastically wherever they performed. In Stockholm, King Oscar went to each evening performance. One day the King's messenger came to say that Anna's presence was requested at the palace. A royal carriage arrived for her, and as Anna later told her friends, "I drove through the streets of the capital as if I were a real princess! The King received me in an immense room. . . . He made a little speech, very kind and charming, to thank me for all the pleasure which my dancing has given him."

The people of Sweden were as delighted as their King. One night after a performance, the audience streamed into the street and escorted Anna's carriage to her hotel. They walked in silence, rich aristocrats side by side with working people, dressmakers, shopkeepers.

Anna went up to her room. Moments later, someone came to tell her that the crowd would not leave until she came out on her balcony. As she opened the balcony doors, a storm of applause and "Hurrahs!" greeted her. She bowed, the crowd shouted more loudly. She bowed again, and they began to sing Swedish songs in her honor.

She wanted to tell them all how moved she was by their kind reception, but what to say? Instead, she went into her room and brought out the baskets of flowers that had been given to her that night in the theater. She threw down roses, lilies, violets, lilacs. At last the mass of people reluctantly departed.

Back in the room Anna asked the maid, "What have I done to evoke such enthusiasm?"

"Madam," the young girl answered, "you have made them happy by letting them forget for an hour the sadness of life."

Thin as a Skeleton

"*. . . forget for an hour the sadness of life.*" It was a phrase that became a part of Anna. She felt herself driven to dance, and she had a goal. "I want to dance for everybody in the world," she said . . . and she nearly did.

When Anna first traveled abroad, Sergei Diaghilev, a promoter of the arts in Russia, was also showing the world the culture of their homeland. In Paris he organized exhibitions and concerts of Russian paintings and music.

Diaghilev had been somewhat surprised at the success of Anna's tour of northern Europe. He hadn't thought that ballet would be popular outside Russia. He knew that audiences in Paris seemed to have lost interest in classical dance. One evening in conversation with Diaghilev and Dandré, Anna suggested that along with painting and music he bring Russian ballet to Paris. Not long after Diaghilev returned to France, Anna received the following telegram:

Committee approves of ballet, but insists that you appear in it. Returning immediately. Sergei Diaghilev.

But Anna had made her own plans. With permission from the Tsar to perform outside Russia, Anna Pavlova and a small troupe of the Imperial Russian Ballet scheduled a tour of Europe. Although she wanted to perform with Diaghilev's company, Anna felt she couldn't break her other commitments. Instead, she promised to join Diaghilev after she had completed her own engagements.

On tour in Berlin, Anna arose one morning to read a critical newspaper review not of her performance, but of herself:

The prima ballerina, Anna Pavlova, whose name was printed in fat letters on the program, is as thin as a skeleton. . . . Although her tip-toe technique is brilliant and her movements are sure, one cannot get any aesthetic enjoyment out of her dancing because of her appearance.

Anna was not deterred by criticism. "I do not dance for the critics, but for this one who is poor, or that one who is sick or worried or has some-body sick at home."

On the same tour, she and her troupe per-formed in Prague, Leipzig, and Vienna. Audi-ences wildly applauded her "tip-toe technique," and many felt her slender physique conveyed an extraordinary grace.

In Paris, Diaghilev had advertised his new bal-let season with a poster sketch of Anna dancing in Fokine's *Chopiniana*. The ballet was reworked and renamed *Les Sylphides* for the new presen-tation.

The St. Petersburg circle of artists and friends worked together on the Paris premiere of the Russian ballet — Fokine as choreographer, and Benois and Bakst designing costumes and scen-ery. Vaslav Nijinsky, an astonishingly talented male dancer, and the young ballerina Tamara Karsavina were leading dancers in the company, although at this time Diaghilev considered Anna his premiere dancer. One critic wrote, "Pavlova, in the opinion of all who saw her, was a second Taglioni." No comment could have pleased Anna more.

After Paris, Anna looked for new audiences. She had briefly visited London on a trip several years earlier, but she hadn't yet danced for an English audience. With her international fame

Anna Pavlova: Genius of the Dance

growing, Anna returned to London at the invitation of Lord and Lady Londesborough to dance at a reception at their home. She was told the King and Queen of England would be present.

Anna's dancing partner for her debut before English royalty was Mikhail Mordkin, a dancer from Moscow. They performed three numbers, the last of which was called *Russian Dance*. Anna wore a national costume, a full-length cloak-dress of white and gold, called a sarafan. An elaborately jeweled headpiece, shaped like a quarter moon, framed her face.

At the end of the program the King and Queen applauded enthusiastically. Lady Londesborough went up to Anna and told her the royal couple wished to meet her. Anna stood at the edge of the platform stage, unable to get down easily in her long costume. King Edward immediately approached and helped her.

Then, as the royal couple were leaving, the band began to play a South American tune called "Paraguay," music Anna had danced to hundreds of times. The Queen turned to her and said, "I know this air so well," and then she asked if Anna would dance to it.

Interviewed by a newspaper reporter the next day, Anna described what happened:

Thin as a Skeleton

Quickly I tied a red 'kerchief round my head,
for local color's sake — "Paraguay" being
really a Spanish dance — and I did my best.
I at once forgot my fatigue; and although I
had been performing for over one hour, I
think I danced better than I ever did before.

Debut in America

Anna's fame was growing. After the gala performance at the Londesborough home, she signed a contract to perform at the Palace Theatre in London the following spring. But first, she returned to St. Petersburg to perform once again in the Tsar's theaters. In November, 1909, she danced at her ten-year benefit performance at the Maryinsky Theater. Flowers filled the stage, and she was given magnificent jewelry, elegant vases, and other beautiful artwork. "To a Divine Talent," read the inscription on a gift wreath.

But Anna needed to travel, to find other worlds in which to dance. In February, with permission of the Tsar, she left the Maryinsky season early and sailed from England on her first trip to America. She and Mikhail Mordkin were scheduled to perform at the Metropolitan Opera House in New York City, and then travel north to Boston and south to Baltimore.

It was a cold February day when Anna and Mordkin arrived in New York. Although New

Yorkers had read that a world-famous ballerina was to dance at the Opera House, few had seen classical ballet except as a short piece during an opera production. In fact, many people called ballet "visual opera."

The director of the Metropolitan Opera House didn't particularly like classical dance. He scheduled Pavlova and Mordkin's debut as the last piece after a full-length production of a long opera. Even though the hour was late, few people left. Reporters, though, were getting restless. Their newspaper deadlines were passing, and still the Russians hadn't appeared.

At last, shortly before midnight, the lights dimmed again and the ballet began. As Anna danced to the music of the ballet *Coppélia,* the applause was thunderous. The last curtain call was at one o'clock in the morning. The next day the headlines read:

ANNA PAVLOWA
A WONDERFUL DANCER
LITTLE RUSSIAN, LITHE,
EXQUISITELY FORMED,
CAPTURES METROPOLITAN
AUDIENCE IN FIRST WALTZ
Her Technique of a Sort to Dazzle the Eye,
And She Has Grace and Humor

The opera production itself was barely talked about. Sol Hurok, the great American organizer and manager of theatrical productions, said Pavlova's first appearance in New York City was the "beginning of the ballet era in our country."

During her days in New York, reporters crowded the stage door and hovered in the lobby of her hotel. Anna was interviewed endlessly. Her name was spelled many ways — Pavlowa, Pavlouva, Pavlow, Pavlov, or Pavlova — "Take your choice," wrote one reporter.

Unaccustomed to writing about dance, the reporters struggled to describe to the general reader what they had seen. "Like the motion of light itself," one wrote. "Fluid loveliness," said another. One critic seemed almost to describe a supernatural creature:

She swooped into the air like a bird and floated down. . . . At times she seemed to defy the laws of gravitation. The Divertissement ended with Pavlova, supported by Mordkin, flying through the air, circling his body around and around. The curtain fell. The applause was deafening.

Anna did have a sense of humor about herself and all the praise she was receiving. One reporter during an interview sighed and murmured that no doubt she ate rose petals. Anna looked at him, paused, and then replied, "I prefer German cooking."

Anna was learning English, and she didn't hesitate to try this new language at every opportunity. You learn from your mistakes, she always said. She spoke rapidly and with a heavy Russian accent most people found charming. "I find it most difficult to understand English, though not so hard to speak it," she told one reporter. Fluent in French, she often gave interviews in that language.

Anna tried to explain to the interviewers the hard work involved in being a dancer. "There are a thousand and one things you just keep thinking of in dancing," she said.

The slightest motion, the least gesture must have its purpose and its meaning. You must manage your breath with more care than a singer. You must be paying attention to the position of your toes, to the motion of your arms, to the expression on your face. And all that is only a little of it. There are rehearsals and rehearsals and still more rehearsals. And when there are no more rehearsals, there are the performances. Yes, it means work, and a good deal of it.

Anna and Mordkin seemed inexhaustible. They danced at charity benefits and special concerts as well as their regularly scheduled performances. Sometimes they worked from mid-afternoon until the early morning hours. From the time Russian dancers are students in the Imperial Theater Schools, they are brought up in a tradition of generosity with their art. In their short stay in America, Anna and Mordkin gave four different charity performances. They even delayed their return date to England to dance at a benefit for the Widowed Mothers' Fund in New York.

In April, Anna and Mordkin finally set sail for England. For Anna it was the beginning of a pattern she was to repeat for many years — two months each year performing in Russia, a stay in London, a tour of the English provinces, and a trip to America.

An Impossible Woman

Anna was nervous about her opening at London's Palace Theatre. Although she had performed before the King and Queen of England at a private party, this was her first appearance before the English public.

The Palace Theatre was a music hall, and Anna had never performed in this kind of theater. Friends had strongly advised her not to appear on such a stage. They said it wasn't "good enough" for her art. But Anna was determined to dance before large audiences.

An evening's performance on the Palace stage might include jugglers, magicians, comedians, and bicyclists. The audience for this sort of entertainment wasn't used to seeing a classical dance program. Would they jeer? Would they sit silently and sullenly? Would they politely but coldly applaud and wait for the next act?

Anna waited in the wings as the music for her duet with Mordkin began to fill the vast theater.

"I stood on the stage before my first English audience, trembling with excitement," she said.

For one of their numbers, she and Mordkin had selected the "Autumn" section from *The Seasons*. "Like a wind-blown flame," one person described their intense and rapid movements. The audience watched in silence. Anna said, "They seemed not to care. . . . I began to fear failure."

At the end of the dance, Mordkin flung Anna to the ground. The audience gasped almost as one. Surely she was injured from such a violent movement! Anna turned her head, smiled, and rose. As she later described it:

> At last I stopped and there was a moment of silence, during which the whole world seemed to stand still. Then, suddenly, the whole theater was clapping, shouting. . . . I cried, I laughed, I held out my hands to them, for I knew I had conquered!

Ten curtain calls later, she and Mordkin at last left the stage.

In the spring of 1910, London had several Russian artists performing at different theaters. So many, in fact, some called it the "Russian Season." But Anna Pavlova was the biggest hit. Newspaper columns began: "Have you seen Pavlova?" Many who had, returned again and again, dazzled by the brilliance of her artistry. Anna became so popular, one restaurant had a new dish

on its menu: "Frogs' Legs à la Pavlova." Mordkin, apparently jealous of all the attention to
Anna, pounded his fist on the table and demanded
to know why there were no "Frogs' Legs à la
Mordkin."

Anna was happy to perform in London theaters
because from her good salary, she was able to
pay her company and buy all their costumes. She
earned additional money by performing at garden
parties in private homes. Until the outbreak of
the First World War in 1914, Anna supported
her company, dancing every spring and summer
in England for sixteen to twenty weeks.

Although Anna herself was earning a good living, she hadn't lost her concern for the problems
of workers who were less well paid than she. One
day when she didn't appear for a rehearsal, the
theater management sent people out to look for
her. Strikes in London had stopped some of the
trains and buses. Anna, no doubt remembering
the strikes in St. Petersburg, was found standing
with a crowd, listening intently to a speaker de-
fend the rights of working people.

Victor Dandré was Anna's constant compan-
ion, managing her business affairs and organizing
all the travel of the Pavlova company. At first
Anna and Dandré stayed at a hotel in London.
But Anna was happiest when she could hear
birds, plant flowers, and walk among the trees.

She and Dandré searched for a house to rent.
Later they bought a large house that no one had
lived in for several years. The house was surrounded by a stone wall covered with ivy, and
ivy also grew in abundance on one of the walls
of the house itself. "Ivy House," as it was called,
sat on a hill. From the balconies, Anna could see
woods, fields, and meadows for miles. She en-
larged the small pond on the land, and it became
the home for two swans she received as a present.

Anna spent a great deal of time in her garden,
lying in a hammock, watching and talking to the
birds, and enjoying her gardens. One morning
when she was awakened early by the sound of
the lawn mower, she ran out to stop the gardener.
"Paul!" she exclaimed. "Do let the daisies live a
little." And once she wrote to him: "I am going
on an extended trip and I forgot to tell you that
it would be very nice if the earth between the
second and third tree on the right side of the
garden could be laid bare by removing the stone
steps. Once this is done the soil there can
breathe."

For a number of years Anna continued to keep
up her apartment in St. Petersburg even though
she lived there only a few months a year. She
brought furniture from that apartment to Ivy
House, and then Anna and Dandré began to ren-
ovate their English home. They built a large stu-

dio two stories high, with a practice *barre* along two walls. A balcony ran around the whole room at the second-story level. Anna's bedroom on the second floor opened onto the studio balcony.

The studio was Anna's work space and also a rehearsal hall for the company. For all the years to come of world traveling, Ivy House was to be home base for Anna and her company. The scenery, trunks of costumes, boxes of wigs, and bins of music for their tours were all kept in stone cellars under the house.

Taking advantage of beautiful summer weather, Anna and Dandré decided to give a housewarming party at Ivy House on a June afternoon. They decked the whole house in garlands of flowers, and invited four hundred guests to an afternoon tea. Anna circulated from table to table, talking with everyone. It was an elegant afternoon, the ladies in splendid frocks and the men in silk hats and finely styled jackets.

In the early evening as the sun was setting, Anna disappeared into the house. Moments later she reappeared in a shepherdess costume, emerging from behind a bush. Her new partner, Laurent Novikoff, in a shepherd's costume, entered with her, and they danced a pas de deux before a delighted audience. The Palace Theatre orchestra accompanied the dancers.

In the following days and weeks, Anna re-

ceived many invitations to parties, but she turned
them all down. She had never much liked society
parties. Newspaper headlines at the time were
calling her "The Dancing Revelation of the Age,"
and "The Incomparable Pavlova." But Mrs. As-
quith, the wife of the English Prime Minister, so
distressed that Anna was turning down all the
social invitations, privately called her "an impossible woman."

"We are not performing tricks!"

" . . . I want to found a school of dancing in London. I want to train some English children. . . . I will be with them and see their talent grow," Anna told a friend. And so she advertised in the London newspapers announcing the establishment of a school at her home. Some parents traveled long distances to bring their children to audition for the class. One young girl, Muriel Stuart, who later danced with Anna's company, took a train, bus, subway, and then walked up a steep hill to reach Ivy House.

Anna selected girls between the ages of nine and thirteen to study with her. When Muriel Stuart auditioned before Anna, she felt completely inadequate. She had taken ballet lessons, but had not learned to dance on pointe or work at the barre. Anna was not concerned. "Sweetly she called me to her," Muriel recalled, "and seemed amused that I could not do any barre work, nodded her head, and said, 'Good, good! I will teach you. You have no bad habits or mannerisms,' kissed me and told me to go home."

Classes began in the morning after Anna had finished her own exercise routine. The students worked in Anna's studio and practiced the ballet positions and simple steps. When she wasn't demonstrating, Anna often sat, sipping a glass of milk, as she watched them work. Anna trained the girls slowly, for young bodies, as she knew from her own teachers, can be harmed if forced to do certain movements before they are strong enough. At first, for example, a young dancer can't stand up on the tips of her toes for even a minute. But slowly the muscles in the toes strengthen so that she can take a few steps. Then more, until she can dance on pointe.

One morning Anna noticed that one of the students was struggling to stand on pointe. The child's mother had apparently taken her to extra classes with another teacher because she thought her daughter was learning too slowly. In a fit of anger, Anna threw down her glass of milk. After tears, explanations, hugs, and a lecture on proper teaching and learning, the students understood why "Madame," as they called her, had become so angry.

Anna had her moods, and the students learned to see them coming. "We knew," said Muriel, "that we should have a terrible time if she appeared in black, a happy one if she was in white!" On "black" days, Dandré often brought a piece of fruit or a glass of milk for the student who was having a particularly hard time.

When Anna was in her dark moods, the students felt terrible for not being able to please her. On her sunny days, they thrilled at the smile or nod of approval she gave, for they adored Madame. As a break from practice, Anna would sit them down for a talk on art in general, and ballet in particular.

"Don't give slavish imitations of the great dancers," she would instruct. "Your interpretation may not be so fine as theirs, but it is better to express oneself even indifferently than to be a mere automaton."

Observation was a key to learning, she told them. It was living homework: "Soon you will be going home on the train. Observe carefully, and try to understand the people you see. . . . Why is that person sad? Perhaps she has to work very hard. Who is that elderly man? What do you get from watching him?"

If you look carefully, Anna would say, you will see how the happy person holds his or her head. You will see the bearing of the shoulders on a sad person. Dance, after all, she explained, is the expression of fact and emotion through movement. You cannot speak of pain, you must show it. You cannot shout, I'm happy! You must move it. "Until you *feel*," she said over and over, "you will never be an artist, only a good machine."

At last Anna felt her students were ready to perform with her at the Palace Theatre. She herself had danced small parts when she was a student at the Imperial Theater School in St. Petersburg. Now she was choreographing for her own students in London. The most exciting part of the program for the young dancers was when they performed with Madame. The dance was called *La Naissance du Papillon* (*Birth of the Butterfly*). Anna, of course, was the butterfly, and her students were seven flowers that surrounded her — a bluebell, buttercup, clover, cornflower, daisy, lily of the valley, and a poppy.

Anna taught her students more than the steps and movements of ballet. You must "reach out" to someone in the audience. "Something must impel you to move. It must be *for* someone. It must not be mechanical. The movement must come from a feeling within you. . . . We are not performing tricks! Those we can see at the circus."

The second year of her Ivy House classes, Anna again brought her students to the Palace Theatre to perform. This time they had a surprise for her. During the program, they came onstage and presented her with a gift, a silver-plated box inscribed, "To Madame Anna Pavlova, from her

"We are not performing tricks!"

loving and devoted pupils, London, August
1913." The names of the seven young performers
were engraved on the box, and in one of the
drawers were seven silver hearts, each inscribed
with one of the girls' names.

A Lump of Cold Cream

"I am only afraid," Tsar Nicholas II told Anna when she left on her first trip to Europe, "lest foreign countries should entice you away from Russia for too long." A few years later, Anna fulfilled the Tsar's prophesy. She wrote to a friend, "I have always secretly dreamed of spending the second half of my career abroad, and it has turned out that way."

After her first visits to England and America, Anna and her company toured the English provinces and the United States nearly every year until the onset of World War I. The travel schedule was often grueling. The company performed eight to eleven times a week, mostly in what were called one-night stands. After an evening performance in one town, the company would board a train and travel through the night to the next city or town for one or two performances the next day. And by nightfall they'd all be back on the trains.

The packing and transport of the baggage was a tremendous feat. Tours across America often

Pavlova at age fifteen, a ballet student in St. Petersburg.

As Princess
Florine in
*The Sleeping
Beauty.*

Maryinsky Theater,
St. Petersburg.

In *Giselle*, Act II, 1903.

Pavlova with teacher Enrico Cecchetti, St. Petersburg, 1906.

139. PREMIÈRE AFFICHE DES « BA

Sketch of Pavlova in *Chopiniana*, used for poster announcing the Russian Ballet's 1909 Paris season.

Pavlova and Stowitts in *Syrian Dance*, 1917.

La Fille mal gardée, 1909.

In costume for *Russian Dance*, 1910.

Pavlova and Michel Fokine in *Cleopatra*, 1911.

In *The Dying Swan*, 1914.

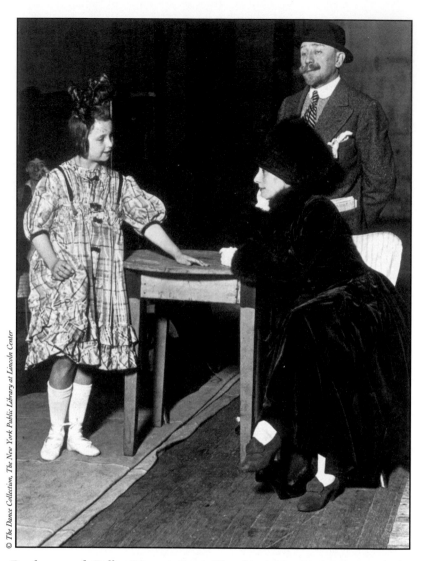

Pavlova and Ballet Master Ivan Clustine interviewing prospective student for Pavlova's ballet school in New York, 1916.

As Aurora in *The Sleeping Beauty*, 1916.

As Fenella in the movie *The Dumb Girl of Portici*, 1915.

Children greeting Pavlova, New York, 1923.

Pavlova with "Jack."

Pavlova arriving
with Victor Dandré
in South America,
1928.

Pavlova with
Japanese teacher,
Kikugoro,
and his family,
1922.

Trip to the Sphinx, Egypt, 1923.

Backstage at the Theatre des Champs Elysées, Paris, 1924.

lasted twenty or twenty-five weeks. On such a trip there were sometimes four hundred pieces of luggage, including at least forty cases of scenery, each weighing hundreds of pounds. There were baskets, boxes, crates, and trunks of costumes, practice clothes, shoes, wigs, music, electrical gear, and the personal luggage of the troupe.

The company performed more than one hundred different dances, some full ballets, some *divertissements*, and each dance had different costumes and scenery. In total, there were probably more than two thousand costumes. Anna's wardrobe designer and his helpers carried their own sewing machines in order to repair torn costumes and make new ones. The company also carried electric heaters, for during the winter months, they sometimes performed in unheated theaters.

Dandré had worked out a swift procedure to transport the enormous load from place to place. Any scenery and costumes that weren't to be used for a particular performance were left at the railroad station. Of course if there was a problem and Anna decided to change the program, someone would rush to the station to search through the trunks for the necessary costumes and scenery.

When everything went on schedule, the procedure worked like this: During each intermission, the sets no longer needed were taken down, packed, and loaded on trucks to be sent to the station. The moment a dancer was off stage, she or he quickly changed into the next costume and dropped the used costume, shoes, and wig into separate open boxes that were quickly filled. Trucks moved back and forth from the theater to the station, carrying the loads as they were ready. After the last intermission, the only thing left in the dressing area was a lump of cold cream on a piece of paper, and a towel to wipe off makeup.

At times there was an odd addition to the transported baggage — a stage floor of sorts. The ideal floor for dances is made of smooth, unfinished pine. Highly polished hardwood, plastic, or linoleum floors are too slippery to dance on. When dancers turn or land from a jump, they have to "feel" the floor under their feet. If it is a polished, glasslike surface, they are likely to slip and fall.

One theater management, trying to be helpful, polished the stage floor until it shone. Understanding they meant well, Anna laughed when she saw it. Then she insisted that stagehands sandpaper it completely. The performance that night was twenty minutes late.

Anna never knew what kind of surface the stage would have as she traveled from town to town. One time when the floor was extremely slick, many in the company wet their shoes, hoping to get a better grip. They still repeatedly fell throughout the performance. Anna, absolutely desperate, put honey on her shoes to make them a little stickier. Algeranoff, one of the company dancers, said nothing really helped. "We went down like ninepins . . ."

Sometimes stage floors had broken boards or holes. Once during an American tour, Dandré had a portable floor made of fitted boards nailed to a cloth. The cloth could be rolled up into a gigantic tube for transport. When Anna tried to dance on it, the "grip" was fine, but it didn't feel like a floor to her. After a short while, the company discarded it.

Dandré then came up with another solution — a heavy linen carpet that could be stretched tightly across the floor. That carpet prevented many a broken bone. Stagehands would make chalk circles on the material to show where the holes underneath were. The dancers could then avoid those spots. Often you'd hear a stagehand yell, "Hey, you, come and do us a pivot and see if this cloth is taut enough!" One of the dancers would then "pivot" until the carpet was nailed down properly. During one performance as Anna stepped on a floorboard, it cracked under her, leaving a gaping hole. Only the linen carpet saved her from falling through.

That all this baggage, including portable floors,

was transported hundreds of thousands of miles without major problems, was a testament to ingenuity. It was a movement of the vast supplies of an army of artists that would have made any general proud.

"You are all my children"

"Madame," company members called her, except, that is, the Russian dancers who in the form used in their own language addressed her by her full name, "Anna Pavlova." Some in the company called her "Madame X." Hilda Butsova, who danced with the Pavlova company for more than thirteen years, said, "I don't know how it began. It seems strange, for X always means the unknown, the mystery. Perhaps she was that too. We knew her; yet we did not know her."

For many years, audiences reading a program at one of Anna's performances might well have thought everyone in the company was Russian, for everyone, it seemed, had a Russian name. In fact, English, Polish, Italian, American, and Australian dancers were all members of the company.

When Anna had returned to England from her first extended American trip, she was excited about introducing her English dancers to an English audience. Newspaper and magazine critics, however, said that the British public wasn't interested in English dancers. They wanted to see the Russians. And so to join Anna's company, a dancer had to "Russianize" his or her name.

One of Anna's leading ballerinas was a fine English dancer named Hilda Boot. To the public she was Hilda Butsova. Algernon Harcourt Essex was a young Englishman who auditioned for Anna at Ivy House. He was offered a contract to join her company, but Algernon was under twenty-one at the time and needed his parents' consent. He would not have been accepted into the company if his mother hadn't agreed to change his name. Algernon became Algeranoff, just as a young Australian man named Arthur was transformed into the Pavlova company dancer named Arthuroff.

Anna's company ranged in size from forty-five to as many as sixty-four people. The number depended on how much money Anna had for salaries, and how long and far the company was to travel. Usually there were at least thirty-two dancers, including Anna's principal male partner, a second ballerina, other classical dancers, the corps de ballet, and so-called "character" dancers for mime parts and national and folk dances.

Few members of an audience ever think about behind-the-scenes staff, but without them there would be no show. People will say, "Wasn't she lovely!" about a particular dancer. In fact, the talent and skill of the dancer are just a part of the total effect. Choreography, music, lighting, costume, set design, makeup, and hairstyle, all are essential to the overall production.

In Anna's company, four or five people worked on wardrobe. They were in charge of designing, sewing, repairing, packing, and unpacking all the costumes. Other people handled wigs and helped the dancers with fixing their hair. Mechanics, electricians, stagehands, and one or two musical conductors were members of the company as well. Usually three musicians — a pianist, violinist, and cellist — traveled with Anna. Crucial to the whole was the ballet master, who directed the production, led the daily classes and rehearsals, and sometimes choreographed new dances.

Early in her career Anna had decided that ballet was to be her life. ". . . artists who are really devoted to their art should not think of marriage," she said. An artist must commit time, energy, all one's thoughts and ideas to her or his art. That would leave little room for attention to a husband or wife or children. But later in life, Anna did marry Victor Dandré, her long-time friend and general manager of her company. Some people believe they exchanged vows during a trip in the United States, but no one knows exactly when, for it was a private affair.

But Anna knew she would not have children. "It is useless to dabble in beauty," she said. "One must be utterly devoted to beauty, with every nerve of the body." A true artist, she used to tell her dancers, is always striving for more beauty. One could not be an artist devoted to one's work and a parent devoted to a child at the same time. It would not be fair either to the work or to the child.

For Anna, the company was her family, and mother them like a family she did. She sometimes said to them, "You are my children." If any member was ill, her concern knew no bounds. She sat with them while they took medicine, made tea, and gave them money for any additional medical needs. Concerned if she thought any of "her family" was unhappy, Anna would rush to find out what was wrong. Problems with a friend? Family trouble? Money difficulties? Anna wanted to know and to help.

Like many a parent, Anna believed her company members should exercise their minds as well as their bodies. It was important, she said, to read good books and magazines. On long train rides, she would walk down the aisle to see what everyone was reading. She approved of only one of the many popular magazines at the time, the *Saturday Evening Post*. Fortunately for company members, it was a magazine large enough to hide other things inside it. As she made her way through the train, Anna nodded and smiled as a sea of *Saturday Evening Posts* appeared in front of her.

Anna wouldn't allow anyone to say or do anything disrespectful of ballet. If a dancer was sloppy in her work, that was disrespect, and Anna wouldn't tolerate it. "You must not be tired," she said. "The audience has a right to be tired because they have been working all day at jobs they don't like, but we are artists, and have to help them get over their fatigue."

Anna taught her dancers the way she had taught her young students, with words and by example. She often said, "Where there is no heart there is no art." If she saw a dancer working only on technique and not working to express feeling, Anna would become angry. "Is this Madame Pavlova's company or a circus?" she once asked a dancer. "How many times have I told you that no real artist will turn more than six pirouettes! Do you want to be a ballerina or an acrobat?"

"Master technique," she often said, "and then forget all about it and be natural." If a dancer in the company would begin to imitate Anna in her movements and gestures, Anna stopped it, saying that copying only blocked one's own originality.

Anna was an emotional person, with intense flashes of joy, anger, and sadness. She explained her frequent changes of mood this way:

I was born in St. Petersburg on a rainy day. You know, it almost always rains in St. Petersburg. There is a certain gloom and sadness in the atmosphere of the Russian capital, and I have breathed the air of St. Petersburg so long that I have become infected with sadness.

But Anna was just as quick to laugh as to cry. And she could be critical of herself as well as of an audience. Frequently after a performance she would say, "I know I could have done better." Once after dancing *The Dying Swan*, she was enraged at the audience for clapping. "How dare they applaud like that! I know I danced badly. It is no compliment to an artist. I shall lose all my standards if people aren't more discriminating." Her company learned to respect high standards in general and Madame's in particular.

On one trip, the company arrived in Washington, D.C., for a three-day engagement. The ballet master, named Pianovski, did not post a rehearsal schedule for the first day. The dancers in the corps de ballet arrived just in time for the performance. The stage was set for the opening ballet. Anna entered from the wings.

"Have you practiced today?" she asked, glancing down the line of dancers who stood ready to perform.

"No," each one murmured. After a long silence, Anna strode to the center of the stage. "I am Anna Pavlova. You are my corps de ballet. I practice every day while you do nothing. We will have a lesson here and now!"

"But Madame," pleaded Pianovski, "the curtain is due to go up in ten minutes. Listen! The audience are in their seats."

One cannot dance without rehearsing, Anna believed — it showed disrespect for the ballet. While people in the audience stamped their feet, demanding that the performance begin, Anna held a rehearsal for half an hour. One did not compromise one's art.

"I can offer nothing but my Art"

It was spring 1914, and Anna was on her way to St. Petersburg. Although she didn't know it, this trip was the last time she would ever see her beloved Russia.

Along the way, Anna performed in various European cities. In Germany, the Duchess of Brunswick, the only daughter of the Emperor, Kaiser Wilhelm II, called for a special performance. She had just given birth to a son, and the gala was to be in honor of the baby's christening.

The rules of behavior in the presence of the German monarchs were rigid and strictly enforced. Theodore Stier, Anna's musical conductor, was instructed to begin the overture when the Emperor sat down, not a moment sooner, not a moment later. Stier paid close attention. He had heard the story of a former conductor at the theater who had wiped his glasses at the very moment the Emperor took his seat. As punishment for beginning the music seconds late, he was fired.

At the time of this performance, Anna Pavlova was considered perhaps the world's greatest ballerina. She was certainly the most famous. She finished her first dance, and the hall was silent. After the second dance, again there was no applause.

Then as she crumpled to the floor at the end of her most famous solo, *The Dying Swan,* a voice bellowed, "Wunderbar! Wunderbar! Brava!" The audience, hearing the Emperor's voice, burst into a roar of applause. When the German royal family attended a performance, no one was permitted to applaud unless and until the Emperor had first shown his approval.

After the performance, Anna was invited to the Royal Box to meet with the Emperor and Empress. Later, back in her dressing room, Stier found Anna shaken and depressed. When she had kissed the Empress's glove, she had left a red makeup smear. "I was never so frightened in my life," Anna later told a reporter. "In Russia such an offense would have had very serious consequences."

The world was indeed on the brink of very serious change, but not because of a lipstick stain on an Empress's glove. Shortly after Anna arrived in St. Petersburg from Germany, newspaper headlines throughout Europe were filled with threats of war. To continue traveling outside Russia, Anna needed a passport, which was issued to her in June. But before going abroad, she scheduled a series of performances in her homeland.

Pavlova had brought two English dancers with her to Russia, Hilda Butsova and Madge Crombova. One afternoon, the three ate lunch at an open-air restaurant close to their Moscow theater. Anna walked down to a nearby lake. Hilda and Madge found her intently watching two giant dragonflies as they moved in and around the plants in the water.

"Look at them! Aren't they marvelous?" Anna exclaimed. "I am going to make a dance out of them. You see? Watch!" Her arms and hands moved in rhythm to the insects' flight. The hot sun beat down mercilessly. Hilda and Madge returned to the shade of the restaurant. "Wait — just a little longer," Anna said. "I will come in a minute." Twenty minutes later she was finally persuaded to leave.

Such peaceful lakeside scenes were not to be repeated for many years. On June 28, 1914, Archduke Franz Ferdinand, heir to the Austrian throne, was assassinated in Sarajevo. Within a month, Austria had declared war on Serbia. Days later, Germany declared war on Russia.

At the very moment of the declaration of war against Russia, Anna was on a train traveling through Germany. Her English agent, having lost contact with her, sent telegrams to all her dancers: "Madame Pavlova's whereabouts unknown. Hold yourself in readiness for rehearsals."

Anna's train arrived at the Belgian border just hours after it had been closed to travel. German police climbed aboard and demanded to see everyone's papers. Anna, with her Russian passport, was arrested.

No one knows how long she was in jail. It might have been for several days. There were rumors she had been accused of being a Russian spy. Afterwards Anna herself rarely talked about her experiences. Years later one of her former pianists wrote, "But for the merest of accidents she might have been destined to remain interned throughout the whole of the War period. She managed to get through, but all her luggage and personal effects were detained in Germany."

Some people have suggested that Anna might have tried to contact the Duchess of Brunswick for help in Germany, but no one is certain. Once freed from jail, her train was stopped dozens of times as she traveled through Belgium. Finally given permission to travel on into France, she at last made her way from there to England.

Anna was grateful to be back at Ivy House. At first everyone had predicted that the war would be over by Christmas. But by mid-September so many young soldiers had died, a heaviness hung over the nation. Anna and

Dandré, meanwhile, had very little money. Anna determined that she had to schedule an American tour to raise funds.

Always willing to dance for a charity benefit, Anna gave one last performance at London's Palace Theatre for the British and Russian Red Cross. As part of the advertising for the performance, a program card in Anna's handwriting was printed for distribution. In it she wrote:

> My heart bleeds for the British soldiers and those of my country and their Allies, who are laying down their lives in a common cause. I can do nothing — I can offer nothing but my Art. It is a poor thing when such brave deeds are being done, yet, if you will help me I will do my utmost, give the best that is in me to ease the terrible sufferings of our brave brothers.

Anna and her company were able to contribute a great deal of money to the Red Cross after that benefit.

Then she set sail for America. The war was to keep her from Ivy House for five long years.

All Across America

Anna stood in the wings preparing for her entrance. First she put one foot in the resin box, then the other. Then up on pointe to rub the resin onto the tips of the shoes so she wouldn't slip onstage. Stepping out of the box, she leaned forward, placing her palms to the floor. Then she extended her right leg to the side, toe pointing to the right, and back, in a movement called a *tendu*. The same to the left. Anna was "tuning" her legs, preparing. Her entrance music was about to begin. Quickly she crossed herself. She flung her arms out stiffly behind her, as if to propel herself out of ordinary life and into the world of her art. She emerged from the wings to long applause.

During the early years of World War I, Pavlova and company traveled east to west, north to south, all across America. Anna was driven by her belief that even audiences who had never before seen ballet would respond to its beauty. And so she traveled to hundreds of small towns as well as all the big cities.

Anna performed on the stages of grand opera

houses, magnificent concert arenas, cramped meeting halls, and small high school auditoriums. At times she and her company were surprised and appalled at the physical conditions of some of the theaters in which they were booked. During one evening's performance, lightning flashed through holes in the roof, and rain sat in puddles onstage. Anna turned to her unhappy company.

"Never mind," she said. "These are people who need us, and it gives me more joy to dance for them then at the Metropolitan Opera House." Muriel Stuart remembered Anna telling the company to ". . . imagine that there might be one or several unhappy people in the audience that had come to forget their cheerless lives . . . dance for them and so bring them happiness."

In another theater, the power lines went dead just before the performance was to begin. Stagehands raced to a nearby garage and borrowed several automobiles. Through open doors and windows the cars were positioned to face the stage, and the headlights were turned on. It was the most unusual spotlight ever focused on Anna.

Schools and town halls rarely had facilities for a professional company. Anna and her dancers frequently used classrooms as dressing rooms. Students' desks would be covered with costumes and makeup. When two, three, or even four dancers shared one small space, their costumes took up most of the room.

When the company danced in a church, the audience sat in pews, and Anna used the organ loft as her dressing room. In a banquet hall in another town, it took two to three minutes to walk from the dressing area to the washroom — much too long when a performer is rushing to change makeup for the next dance.

In some halls, the dancers had to change costumes one or two floors above the stage. The race to make a curtain call could be perilous. One night as one dance was ending, someone rushed up the stairs to the balcony dressing rooms that overlooked the stage. "Quick!" he yelled. "Jean's forgot her pants for *Greek*!" which was the next dance on the program. Someone hurled the costume pants over the balcony. They landed in Jean's hands just as the curtain was rising on her number.

In real theaters designed to accommodate performers, there were no such logistic problems. At the end of August, 1916, Pavlova and company began a season of performances at one of the largest theater arenas in the country, the Hippodrome, called "The National Amusement Institution of America." It was an enormous theater in New York City, seating five thousand people, and Anna and her dancers were scheduled to perform there for six months.

Now Anna stood in the wings of the Hippodrome. In a costume of blue, green, and purple net that she had designed, she flitted onto the stage. Wings quivered on her back as her hands fluttered, and her feet darted forward, back, and sideways. Swaying, soaring, she seemed to be in flight. A year earlier in Moscow she had been bewitched by a real dragonfly dance. She had choreographed her own dazzling shimmer of a dragonfly dance from that experience, and now she was dancing it for the first time.

Anna, who had once said she would never share a stage with animals, was now performing on programs with acts that included elephants, acrobats, jugglers, West Point cadets, minstrel singers, and a pianist who played while he and his white piano were flown on wires back and forth across the stage.

The Pavlova company, exhausted from darting in and out of towns across the country, needed to perform in one place for a length of time. Anna also needed money. She had purchased a bankrupt opera company that was now performing with her, and the expenses were enormous.

Anna's first program at the Hippodrome was a production of *The Sleeping Beauty*. Her company and all the other acts on the Hippodrome program rehearsed at an armory building. Many of the other performers had never before seen classical ballet or worked around ballet dancers. Since Anna was to be dancing at the Hippodrome for six months, she decided to introduce herself and her dancers to all the others. At the first rehearsal, she and her new partner Alexandre Volinine danced the pas de deux from *The Sleeping Beauty* for the entire cast. The applause at the end was deafening.

Anna's friend Léon Bakst was now a world-famous designer working in Europe. When Anna agreed to perform at the Hippodrome, Bakst designed and shipped the sets and costumes for *The Sleeping Beauty* to New York, one piece at a time as each was finished.

At the dress rehearsal, the last rehearsal before opening night, it was hard to believe the show would open on schedule. The ballet costumes were not finished. Forty sewing machines buzzed in the lobby of the first balcony as sewers worked all night stitching spangles on Bakst's costumes.

Some of the sets weren't ready, either. Hundreds of performers darted back and forth across the stage, avoiding open trapdoors and swinging stage machinery. Humans squeezed around elephants as they exited from the stage.

But the show did open on time, with Anna a rousing success. "There were many stars, and the greatest of these was Pavlowa, Anna the Great, probably the most famous of woman dancers, certainly the greatest that American theatregoers have seen," wrote the reporter for the *New York Herald*.

Anna worked intensely. Even with her heavy performance schedule, she found time to start another ballet school, this time in America. "It is quite thrilling to have pupils. . . . I don't think an artist can ever do greater service to her generation than to teach the younger folk whatever she has learned by experience and labor."

When Anna advertised she was opening a school, over twelve hundred applicants applied. Children and their parents gathered at the Hippodrome, and Anna and her ballet master, Ivan Clustine, examined them. One young girl, feeling tremendous pressure to perform well, became so upset she sat on the floor and sobbed. Anna picked her up and put the child on her lap. The girl relaxed and was at last able to perform.

Still Anna did more. There were always the charity benefits she could never turn down. At one, funds were raised for the Russian war relief. For another charity, the composer-conductor John Philip Sousa directed an orchestra playing his own music. Anna and Volinine agreed to dance to one of Sousa's waltzes. It was a very long piece, and together with Sousa they worked out a plan to cut the length.

The day of the performance, Anna and Volinine whirled onstage. The time came for the cut, but Sousa played on . . . and on . . . and on. Completely exhausted, the dancers improvised until the piece finally ended. They could barely walk off stage. When Anna saw Sousa after the show, she was very angry about his forgetting the cut.

"Madame," he explained. "I did not forget it, but I was so happy that Pavlova was dancing my favorite waltz, that it was quite beyond my power to end it so quickly."

". . . almost as prisoners"

By the time of her last performance at the Hippodrome in January, 1917, over seven million people had seen Pavlova dance there. Soon millions more would see "The Incomparable Pavlova" and her Russian ballet.

"You have done fine work these last months," Anna told the company at the New Year's party in her New York apartment. "But now we go to a new continent, and everyone must work very, very hard, so these people may see the Russian Ballet at its best!" And with that, Anna announced a tour of South America.

After a series of performances in Cuba and Costa Rica, the company sailed for Ecuador. The trip should have been a warning of what was to come. They traveled by cattle boat, and the passenger deck was just above the cattle. The noise and smell from the lower deck were overwhelming. The weather was so hot and sticky, most of the company slept on deck. Anna would walk the deck at night trying to cheer everyone up. They loved her for trying, and sympathized when she shuddered at the loud moaning of the cattle. The odors finally drove her back to her cabin.

As the boat drew near the dock in the town of Guayaquil, company members could see people in rags staring up at them. The houses on the hill looked as poor as the people. The first rehearsal was equally depressing. The theater was dark and dirty. When the doors opened for the first performance, most of the audience coming in was barefoot. Classical ballet was totally unknown in these parts, yet Anna danced as if the Tsar and Empress were seated in a royal box looking down on the stage. The audience was fascinated and delighted.

The poverty of the people and the diseases that had infected so many of the locals wore down the dancers' spirits. Even Anna seemed to lose hope. She felt trapped and actually began to believe they would never leave Guayaquil alive. At last the ship arrived to take them to Lima and what many felt was the real beginning of their Latin American tour — Peru, Chile, Argentina, Brazil, Venezuela, and back again.

Thrilled to have left Ecuador, the company enjoyed the next months. The last night in Lima, the president of Peru attended the show. At the end, ballet lovers in the audience released dozens of caged birds into the air. The stage was knee-deep with flowers. "Adios!" the audience shouted over and over again. Hundreds waited by the theater doors. Anna had tears in her eyes as she made her way through the crowd.

But there were also difficult times. In Venezuela the president of the country wanted to see the ballet *Coppélia*. In order to perform this ballet, the orchestra would have had to rehearse on a Sunday morning. The musicians refused. Many of them were playing in churches that day. The president was outraged that he wasn't getting his way. He ordered the orchestra members to rehearse, or be shackled in chains and jailed for six months.

Anna was a world-famous star, and she expected to be treated with respect. But it was her art, not her person, she believed was most important. Although she had become accustomed to publicity, Anna had an intense reaction the first time she saw an ad about herself. Before the war, on top of a bus in London, was a sign written in huge letters: "ANNA PAVLOVA." Anna burst into tears on seeing it. It was undignified, she thought, for an artist to be advertised like a can of soup.

Now, years later in Brazil, Anna's sense of what was proper was again jarred. At the end of her stay in one city, local officials organized a reception in her honor. The town council had a marble plaque designed and mounted on the wall of the theater. "ANNA PAVLOVA DANCED IN THIS THEATRE," it read. Anna was so up-set, she said she was too ill to go to the reception. The plaque violated her sense of what was fitting. Such things, she told Dandré, should not be done during the life of an artist.

Although far from the battlefront, the company still felt the effects of the war. The dancers carried passports from many different countries. Some of the Latin American nations supported Britain, France, and Russia in the war. Others backed Germany and Austria. The company was stopped and questioned extensively at some borders. In Brazil, one of the dancers was imprisoned for carrying an "enemy" passport, even though he hadn't been back to his homeland for fifteen years.

Despite all the war tension, Anna was deter-mined to perform on schedule. "I have many friends lost in the war . . . and often when I must dance, I am sad," she once explained. "Tonight I have a letter from a dear friend in London. Her husband is just killed in the war. He, too, was my friend. But one must think of the people out in front, so that you not make them sad too, is it not so?" As Anna traveled down the coast of South America, she gave a benefit performance for the Red Cross in each city.

While Anna was touring, the news from her homeland shocked her. The Tsar had been overthrown, and a new Soviet government was in power. It was seven years before Anna learned that her mother was alive and safe in the city of Odessa. News from her home in London, however, was more satisfying. Ivy House was being used as a hospital for wounded soldiers.

While on tour, Anna worked for the armed forces in yet another way. In the Panama Canal Zone, she danced for American marines and naval personnel on a stage specially built for her at a pier. Scenery was hung from the warehouse girders, and travelers were able to peer into the warehouse as their steamers passed by. Anna insisted that the prices be kept low, and thousands of people bought tickets. The earnings were donated to the Red Cross.

Finally the war was over. But Anna had signed contracts for additional tours in Mexico and South America. She couldn't go home until that schedule was completed. Of the company's travels during the war years, she later said, "We were kept almost as prisoners in South America for years. It was . . . a triumphal tour, but, nevertheless, it lasted too long."

Anna had left Ivy House in October, 1914. She didn't return until March, 1920.

"Fancy, dancing with only one leg!"

When Anna and Dandré first moved to Ivy House, she was given a pair of swans as a gift. Although they were somewhat wild, Anna trained the two to come when she called. "Of my pets," and she had many, Anna said, "the swans are . . . my favorites. They are very fond of me, principally because . . . I feed them cakes and crackers."

Now Anna was back at Ivy House, but the swans didn't answer her call. After all, five and a half years had passed since they had last heard her voice. She felt sad, and talked about the swans to a newspaper reporter. A few days later, she received a letter from a stranger who said he loved swans and thought he could help tame hers again. Anna invited him to Ivy House, and he agreed to work with the swans every day for two to three hours. Anna and Dandré called him "the Swan Professor." Jack, the wilder of the two swans, became so tame with Anna, she could play with him, roughing him up almost as much as she could her dog.

But Anna's work demanded she leave Ivy House again. She scheduled trips to the English provinces, Europe, and toured again in the United States, Canada, Mexico, and South America. As world-famous as she was, there were always new audiences, people who had never seen ballet, or Pavlova, before.

On one trip to Scotland, Vincenzo Celli, a member of her company, rented an apartment in the town where they were performing. When his landlady learned he was a dancer, she was intrigued. She couldn't believe that an entire theater performance could be devoted only to dance, with no speaking parts. Celli showed her a picture of Anna dancing *The Dying Swan*.

"Fancy, dancing with only one leg!" she commented. Anna, when told the story, insisted that Celli bring his landlady to the theater, take her to dinner afterwards, and then tell Anna what she said. The landlady loved the show.

Not all audience members were as pleased with classical dance. In Birmingham, England, a local citizens' committee complained that one of Anna's dancers wasn't wearing tights. The ballet was an Indian national dance, and the dancer was supposed to be bare-legged. A sensational news article about the affair drew comment from all over. Nearly two thousand articles were written about the incident in magazines and newspapers around the world. When the English comedian George Rabey next played in Birmingham, he decided to avoid any possible problem: He put stockings on the legs of the grand piano he used in his act.

In America, Anna spent weeks in California, performing in dance programs and acting and dancing in a film called *The Dumb Girl of Portici*, based on an opera by Auber. In the film, she played the part of Fenella, a mute young woman. During her visits to Los Angeles, Anna had become friendly with many movie stars, including Mary Pickford, Douglas Fairbanks, Rudolph Valentino, Lillian Gish, and Charlie Chaplin. One evening when Anna had invited guests to dinner at a restaurant, Chaplin stood up and did an imitation of her dancing *The Dying Swan*. Anna laughed uproariously along with everyone else. And Chaplin was not the only one to imitate her. During the years of Anna's extraordinary fame, nearly every great comedian did an imitation of her dancing the Swan role.

Anna returned the joke one night in Liverpool. Just before the curtain rose, the corps de ballet was assembled onstage. Anna stood in the wings in a white *tutu*, bobbing up and down, swinging an imaginary cane and lifting and tipping a non-existent bowler hat in imitation of Chaplin. As the curtain rose, the corps members frantically tried to stop laughing.

"Madame herself remained in the wings, cheerfully grinning at our discomfort. For nothing gives you a worse tummy-ache," said Algeranoff, "than trying to dance when you want to laugh."

The post-war period also had its dark side. With the end of the war came frequent news reports of large numbers of Russian children who were orphaned and starving. "The knowledge," Anna said, "was like a knife in my heart." She gave special charity performances to raise funds to send to Russia. In a magazine article she wrote:

> To dance for them! It was such an easy thing. It seemed to me that I should be over there helping them, looking after them, caring for them myself. It was a foolish wish, of course. Naturally the money I could earn for them, dancing, meant a great deal more than my solitary personal services would.

But Anna had an idea for other personal services she could give. In 1921, she rented a house outside Paris, fixed it up, furnished it as a home for exiled Russian refugee girls, and hired staff to take care of the girls. She raised money for the home by giving dance benefits, and also by asking people to contribute. Americans were among the most generous. Businessman Edsel Ford paid all the costs to support one orphan for a whole year.

"Fancy, dancing with only one leg!"

The Campfire Girls of America also made a contribution. They raised one thousand dollars collecting pennies from thousands of children. But Anna never was able to raise enough money for the upkeep of the home, and so she paid for most of the costs out of her own pocket. By the time the home closed years later, some forty-five girls had lived there.

New Worlds, New Ideas, New Ballets

"I am haunted by the need to dance," Anna once said. She might have added, "And to dance, before new audiences." Anna had traveled extensively throughout North America, South America, and Europe, but had not yet been to the Far East. It was her next goal.

With a small company of dancers and musicians, Anna and Dandré set sail for Japan. They were about to begin their Far Eastern adventure. From Japan, Anna traveled on to China, the Philippines, the Malay States, Burma, India, and Egypt.

For the first time Anna was traveling in lands where verbal communication was often difficult. Few natives spoke any of the European languages Anna and her company members knew. In fact, Anna and the others often had to explain their need for stage sets and lighting by improvising in sign language. When Dandré tried to hire orchestra members, he found few local musicians who knew how to play the western music for the ballets in Anna's repertoire. And except for a few people in big cities, the many thousands who watched Pavlova and Company perform had never before seen Western dance. But dance, Anna had always believed, was an international language that crossed geographic borders, language barriers, and cultural differences.

Travel for Anna was a learning experience. On the boat trip to Japan, she told company members she hoped they would explore the different cultures. When they arrived at a new place, Dandré arranged the work and travel schedule so that there were always free days between performances. On these days, Anna visited museums, monuments, art exhibitions, temples, and other places of interest. And she encouraged the company to do likewise.

In Egypt, Anna and some of the dancers saw the Pyramids and the Sphinx. In India, she visited the Taj Mahal in the moonlight and thought it the most beautiful structure she had ever seen. She sat in the garden of the building all through the night. As the morning light appeared, she knew she would create an Indian ballet. When Anna later visited the extraordinary Ajanta caves, a famous Buddhist temple in India where the walls are covered with paintings, the idea for an Indian ballet began to take shape. She made careful notes and drawings and took photographs of the paintings. Back in London, Algeranoff did extensive research for her at libraries and museums. Her ballet *Ajanta's Frescoes* was the result.

Most important to Anna was to see and learn different national dances. She already included in her repertoire Dutch, Persian, Polish, Hungarian, and, of course, Russian national dances. On this trip, Anna looked for teachers in each country she visited.

One day shortly after they arrived in Tokyo, she turned to André Olivéroff, one of her dancers. "Andrusha, listen to me! I am absolutely thrilled about Tokyo, and I cannot wait any longer to explore it a little!" So off they went. When they saw a demonstration of Japanese dancing, she exclaimed, "I must see all the dancing that I can while we are here in the Orient. We must all of us study their dancing. . . . It will be useful for us. I think I must arrange an Oriental ballet." Anna did study with a Japanese teacher, and then created *Oriental Impressions* when she returned home. It is a dance in three parts, two based on authentic Hindu movements and mythology, and one on a Japanese theme. Anna's Japanese teacher was listed in the program notes when she performed this dance.

Anna was often inspired to create a new dance by a thought or event that unexpectedly occurred. She had the idea for her favorite ballet, *Autumn*

Leaves, when she was onboard a ship. Listening to music by Chopin, she began thinking about a young student boyfriend in St. Petersburg years earlier who had drowned. She choreographed a lovely dance of a lone chrysanthemum bloom tossed about by an autumn wind, saved at first, but then finally abandoned, by a young man.

On another occasion, a gift became part of a dance. When she arrived in South Africa, Anna and her company were met by a group of women representing an organization of dance teachers. They presented her with a large fan of ostrich feathers. She promised she'd use that fan in a dance during her stay, and she did.

This sort of inspiration could happen wherever she was. Once when traveling in California, Anna came through a snow-filled mountain pass down into a valley teeming with poppies. Watching them open in the morning with the rising sun and then close at sunset inspired her dance *California Poppy*. Her costume had red petals and a green bodice, and she wore a yellow wig. Anna designed the costume so that she was able to open one petal at a time as the day began, and then close them one by one as the day ended.

As graceful and beautiful to watch as the movements were, that was not Anna's primary purpose. "In creating a ballet," she said, "one must constantly ask not, Is this pretty and graceful? but rather, Does this exactly represent the idea intended?"

The last new continent for Anna to explore was Australia. When she and her troupe arrived in Sydney, ten thousand people gathered at the railroad station to greet her. On the evening of her last performance, showers of paper streamers, colored ribbons, and flower bouquets were tossed on the stage. A young girl stepped forward and handed Anna a boomerang with flowers on it.

"The boomerang comes back," she said, "and we hope you'll come back too!"

Anna also brought some of her own traditions with her when she traveled. She adored Christmas and always wanted to celebrate it as she had as a child, with a tree lit with candles and hung with fruit. Christmas was not Christmas without a tree. Once in Wisconsin, not only did she have a splendid tree, but she also rented a horse-drawn sleigh and took the company on a glorious ride through the woods.

But sometimes she had to improvise. On their trip to Rangoon, she and Dandré could not find a proper tree. She gave a party for the company in the stifling heat, using an artificial fir tree. Electric fans were turned on to cool the room. But Anna had them shut off for a few minutes so she could light the candles. The heat was so great, however, the candles were soon blown out and the fans turned back on.

Anna vowed never again to be without a tree. On her trip to South Africa, she managed to sneak a huge tree on board the ship as a "piece of luggage." When she gathered the company together in the ship's dining room, they were startled to see a beautiful Christmas tree decorated with artificial snow. Only Anna could be counted on to create a white Christmas as they sailed south of the equator.

The Last Dance

"Tell me, Doctor, what must I do?" Anna asked as she waited in the wings for the overture to begin. Her leg was aching badly.

"Madame, you must rest for three weeks."

That was impossible. "I know that, Doctor, but tell me what I must do!" There was no answer. Anna called for a company member, who massaged and strapped her leg. Anna danced that evening and afterwards completed her performance schedule.

Although she was at times ill, rarely did an audience know anything was wrong. When she was performing in St. Louis, Missouri, Anna hurt her left ankle during a rehearsal. Newspaper reporters somehow learned of the accident and asked Anna which ankle was injured. She said, "The right one." Later she told her dancers, "You see, now they will watch the right ankle during the performance, and nothing will seem amiss."

On other occasions, however, Anna could not hide an injury. Shortly after the start of a ballet one evening, Anna fell back, unable to stand on her foot. Some members of the audience said they heard a snapping sound. Doctors disagreed about the diagnosis. One advised an operation, although he said she might never dance again. Another said she shouldn't dance for at least two months. A third recommended special massage treatments. Anna took the massage, and within ten days she was dancing again.

Often she defied sickness and pain in order to perform. One evening Anna had a severe tonsillitis attack. Nonetheless, she insisted on dancing against doctor's orders. As she exited from a curtain call, she babbled feverishly in French about a bouquet of flowers that in fact didn't exist. Conductor Stier, concerned that Anna was not taking care of herself, threw down his baton and said he would play no more until she was well.

Most often Anna didn't listen to doctors when they told her to take a break from dancing and rest. But she did listen to dance criticism. "I have never stopped learning," she said, "and I continue to do so."

One time in Holland, a young dancer in the company had a slight injury and was unable to perform for a while. Anna was rehearsing her role in *La Fille mal gardée*, a classical ballet she had danced in at the Maryinksy Theater in St. Petersburg. Anna put her arm around the young woman's shoulders. "You go in front tonight, yes? I think you go in front, you tell me how it is I dance, and you look at my make-up, and tell me all you think." Later the dancer hesitated as she approached Anna's dressing room, fearful she might anger or upset the world-famous ballerina.

"How did it look to you, my dear?" asked Anna. "What did you think? Was it bad?"

"Well, Madame" — the dancer paused for a moment and then continued — "I have seen you dance better." She explained why and added, "Your make-up made you look about seventeen years old, which of course is quite correct for the part, but I think your eye shadow was a little too heavy."

Anna looked at the girl. "Ah! You think I am bad. Never before has someone told me I am bad." At that moment the young dancer thought she was about to be fired. But Anna continued. "Everybody tells me, 'Madame, you are wonderful, Madame, you are marvelous.' I know this is not true because sometimes I don't feel so good, and I know I don't dance so well. I can't see myself, and so it is difficult to correct what is bad, but now you help. I am pleased."

Anna had signed a contract for a long European tour that began in January, 1930, and ended in Paris in May. By the time the tour was over, Anna was tired. She rested first at Ivy House and then in the south of France.

In the fall, she began a new ballet season in England. One morning while practicing at the barre, she said to one of her dancers, "Nina, please find out if there is a Russian Orthodox Church here. Go and pray for me. I feel so depressed. . . . I feel in the shadow of a heavy, dark cloud." Nina went and prayed.

It was as if Anna had a premonition. Sol Hurok, the American theatrical manager, was in England visiting with Anna and Dandré. He was about to sail for America. Anna was chatting with him, when suddenly she said, "I'm going to see you off at the boat." Both Dandré and Hurok tried to discourage her. "It's so damp at the dock," Hurok said. "You might catch a cold."

"You can both go to the devil!" Anna exclaimed. She looked at Dandré. "Don't you know I may never see him again?" At the boat, she checked Hurok's accommodations and told a ship's officer, "Take good care of my friend Hurokchik." Then she said good-bye.

Anna was scheduled to begin performances in Europe in mid-January, 1931. On the morning of December 14, she left Ivy House for a short vacation in France before the tour was to begin. Usually when she left her home, she went through the entire house and garden, saying good-bye to all her pets, flowers, the trees she loved, and all her favorite possessions. This morning she rushed out of the house without a word to anyone or anything.

New Year's Eve, Anna and Dandré went to a party in Cannes on the French Riviera. She was warmly applauded when she entered the restaurant where the party was being held. It was noisy and hot indoors. The waiter opened a window, and a pigeon flew in, landing on Anna's shoulder. Anna shuddered. There was a Russian superstition that when a bird flies into a room, it is an omen of death. She left the party early and went home.

On January 10, Anna traveled by night train to Paris. She was sleeping when suddenly the train shook violently and came to a sudden stop. Anna put on a light coat over her pajamas. There was snow on the ground, but she climbed down and, with many other passengers, walked along the siding to see what had happened. Her train had collided with another train traveling on the same track. It was many hours before they started up again. Anna stood in the cold for a long time.

After several days of rehearsal in Paris, the company boarded a train bound for The Hague in Holland. Anna was usually the first one to arrive at the train station, but this time no one had seen her. She appeared just as the doors were closing. Her maid and secretary seemed to be holding her up.

Anna shivered as she climbed aboard. After she retired to her compartment, the train stewards were overheard whispering to each other. "She must be very ill," one said. "She was talking without stopping, and sometimes sobbing. And screaming."

When they arrived at The Hague, Anna told the violinist who met them at the station, "I am sorry about the rehearsal tonight. We will have to postpone it. I am not well." Anna had a high fever and was coughing painfully. A doctor, called to her hotel room, concluded there was an inflammation in her left lung.

At times Anna was delirious. Other moments she talked very practically with Dandré about business arrangements and rehearsal schedules. But she wasn't getting any better, and additional doctors were called in. Within days, the inflammation had spread to the right lung. She was told an operation would probably help, but she would never be able to dance again. Anna said no to the operation.

On Monday, January 19, Anna and her company were to begin their tour, but Anna lay in bed having trouble breathing. A newspaper headline across the Atlantic in New York City read, "PAVLOVA MUFFS FIRST DATE IN 30 YEARS."

Algeranoff, who had performed with Anna for

many years, wasn't dancing with the company this trip. The same Monday that Anna's tour was to have started, a wristwatch that Anna had given him stopped working. When he heard that she had cancelled a performance, Algeranoff knew the situation had to be serious, for she always had danced through sickness.

The hotel where Anna was bedridden was wild with activity. Telephone calls from around the world tied up the switchboard. People left cards and messages for her. Some offered to donate blood if she needed it. A Dutch professor and his daughters volunteered to drive throughout the city, running errands for Anna and her doctors. Flowers and newspaper reporters crowded the lobby. Every three hours, the Queen of Holland called to hear the latest medical report.

Anna tossed feverishly in her bed. Then all at once, she sat up and talked about the performance that was to take place in Brussels in two days. It was a benefit to raise money for poor students. She insisted the performance not be cancelled. "My company is the work of twenty years. It must outlive me," she cried.

Midnight on Thursday, January 22, Anna lost consciousness. Her breathing became fainter and fainter. Suddenly she opened her eyes. She seemed to be trying to say something. Her maid, Marguerite, bent over her. "'Get my Swan costume ready," Anna whispered, and then she made her final request. "Play that last measure softly."

Half an hour later, in the early morning hours of Friday, January 23, 1931, Anna Pavlova died.

Anna's coffin was brought back to London. In a Russian Orthodox Church on Buckingham Palace Road, the coffin was draped with an old Russian flag. For a day and a half, thousands of Londoners came to pay their last respects. Enormous wreaths of flowers alongside penny bouquets covered the coffin as flowers so often had covered the stage.

The night after her death, Anna Pavlova's company kept their concert date in Brussels. After the last dance, the orchestra began to play the music for *The Dying Swan*. The curtain rose on an empty stage as the spotlight moved forlornly across the empty boards. The Belgian King Albert and Queen Elizabeth and the entire audience stood.

At a memorial service in New York City, modern dancer Ruth St. Denis said, "Pavlova lived on the threshold of heaven and earth as an interpreter of the ways of God."

Glossary

This is a selected glossary of words used in this book. In 1661, the French King Louis XIV founded the first school of dance in the world. Since then, French words are often used for ballet steps.

Ballerina: A ballerina is the main female dancer of a company. In a large company with more than one ballerina, the *prima ballerina* is the leading ballerina. It takes years of hard work and fine dancing in important roles to become a prima ballerina, and Anna Pavlova was one.

Ballet master: Traditionally, the ballet master was the choreographer who created dances for the company. More recently, the ballet master or mistress may or may not choreograph dances, but usually rehearses, teaches, and assigns roles to company members.

Balletomane: A person devoted to the ballet. The word was first used in Russia to describe the people who attended every performance, sitting in the higher-priced seats called the stalls. The term now refers to anyone who deeply loves the ballet and frequently attends performances.

Barre: The barre is a rail attached to the walls of a ballet studio at roughly waist height. It is used for support during exercises, and is usually held lightly.

Classical ballet: The term usually refers to both the traditional way of training ballet dancers and a number of specific ballets. Pavlova was taught in the classical way and trained her students similarly. Examples of classical ballets are *Swan Lake*, *The Sleeping Beauty*, *The Nutcracker*, and *Giselle*.

Corps de ballet: In most countries, the corps de ballet refers to all the dancers in the company below the soloists.

Coryphée: A coryphée is a leading member of the corps de ballet.

Dacha: A dacha is a Russian country cottage, used most often in the summer.

Danseur: A danseur is a male dancer. A leading male dancer is called a premier danseur.

Divertissement: This usually refers to a collection of dances in classical ballets, such as *The Sleeping Beauty* and *The Nutcracker*, that usually has nothing to do with the rest of the ballet. It is a chance to show off the dancing skills of the principals and soloists of a company.

Fouetté: This is the usual name for a step in which the dancer stands on one leg and uses the other in a whipping motion to help turn the body. It is almost always performed by a female dancer on pointe. In Act III of the classical ballet *Swan Lake*, the Black Swan usually performs this turn thirty-two times.

Icon: An icon is a picture or image. In Eastern Christianity, it is a religious image or portrait, usually of the Virgin Mary, Christ, or a saint or martyr, and is often painted on a wooden panel.

Pas: Pas means step in French. In the ballet, it is used to mean a dance for one or any number of performers, for example, *pas de deux* (dance for two). When Anna Pavlova danced as a member of the Imperial Ballet Company, a pas de deux followed a strict form of choreography that included an entrance for the two dancers, then a solo called a variation for each, and finally the coda, or the end.

Pirouette: This is a complete turn of the body performed on one leg. When dancers perform more than one pirouette, they "spot," which means they fix their eyes on one spot while they turn. As they turn, the head moves last and fastest, and returns quickly to the same spot to avoid dizziness. Female dancers usually turn pirouettes on pointe.

Pointe, pointes: A dancer is on pointe when she stands on the tips of her toes. Danc-

ing on pointe began in the first half of
the nineteenth century, when female
dancers wore soft shoes. In the last half
of the nineteenth century, Italian shoe-
makers began to make ballet shoes with
a stiff, boxed toe, and then dancing on
pointe became popular.

Romantic ballet: The term was originally used
to describe ballets created in the period
between 1830 and 1850, when Marie
Taglioni, Anna Pavlova's idol, was a tre-
mendously popular ballerina. The term is
now used to describe a ballet that is Romantic in mood, and is considered a
form of classical ballet. Several ballets
that Pavlova was famous for, like *Giselle*
and *Les Sylphides*, are considered Romantic ballets.

Samovar: A samovar is a pot or urn with a
spigot, used especially in Russia to boil
water for tea.

Tendu: This is a movement where the foot
slides forward, backward, or to the side
as far as it can go, with the toe never
leaving the floor, and the leg kept
straight.

Glossary

Tutu: The name for the very short, fluffy skirt
worn by ballerinas in classical ballets.
The tutu is the accepted dress for female
dancers even in new ballets choreographed in the classical style.

Selected Bibliography

There are many books written about ballet, and hardly a one doesn't mention Anna Pavlova. Below are a few of the books I have found particularly helpful. Some are more difficult than others, more complex in structure, more detailed in the material presented. All are worth looking at for the sense they convey of the artistic richness of the ballet world and also for the many collections of wonderful photographs. Books specifically written for a young audience are so noted.

Books of memoirs written by people with firsthand knowledge of Pavlova convey a sense of intimacy with the subject. Scholars, however, are often quick to point out errors in memoirs. After all, most people don't keep detailed and careful diaries. And sometimes a person wants to remember something in one way, although what really happened was different. But even when dates or times or places are wrong, a well-written personal story can bring the reader close to the subject.

First-Person Accounts:

Algeranoff, H. *My Years with Pavlova*. London: William Heinemann, 1957. Autobiography of a principal performer in Pavlova's company. Algeranoff danced with Pavlova from 1921 to 1930 and kept a diary of his experiences, relying on that rather than just memory for the writing. Considered to be one of the most accurate of the personal memoirs.

Butsova, Hilda. "My Days with Pavlowa," as told to Courtney Davidge. *The Dance Magazine:* May 1926, Vol. 6, No. 1.

The Dance Magazine. "Pavlowa Section." August 1931, Vol. 16, No. 4. A portion of the magazine devoted to reminiscences of Pavlova upon her death. Includes pieces by former students, dance partners, members of her company, and her husband.

Dandré, Victor. *Anna Pavlova in Art and Life.* London: Cassell & Co., 1932; Arno, 1979. A biography of Pavlova by her husband.

Fokine, Michel. *Fokine: Memoirs of a Ballet Master.* Translator, Vitale Fokine; editor, Anatole Chujoy. Boston: Little, Brown, 1961. An autobiography that includes stories about Anna Pavlova, with whom Fokine danced in the Russian Imperial Ballet, and for whom he choreographed *The Dying Swan.*

Hyden, Walford. *Pavlova.* London: Constable & Co., 1931. Hyden was a pianist and at times musical director for Pavlova, and he traveled with the company on some of their tours.

Karsavina, Tamara. *Theatre Street: The Reminiscences of Tamara Karsavina.* New York: E.P. Dutton, 1931, 1950. Extremely interesting memoir of this prima ballerina's career, including her training at the Imperial Ballet School in St. Petersburg. Karsavina, a few years younger than Pavlova, grew up in the same world as Pavlova and shared many of the same experiences.

Olivéroff, André, as told to John Gill. *Flight of the Swan: A Memory of Anna Pavlova.* New York: E.P. Dutton, 1932. Memoir of an American dancer with Pavlova's company.

Brief memoirs written by Pavlova have appeared in several books and publications. Although very similar, each has some material different from the others. One only wishes she had written more:

Pavlova, Anna. "The Story of My Life," *The Dance Magazine,* April–July, 1928.

———. "Pages of My Life," Franks, A.H., editor. *Pavlova, a Biography,* Chapter 8. London: Burke, 1956.

———. "Towards a Dream of Art," Olivéroff, André, as told to John Gill. *Flight of the Swan: A Memory of Anna Pavlova,* pp. 50–62. New York: E.P. Dutton, 1932.

Other books I found interesting and helpful are:

Balanchine, George, and Francis Mason. *Balanchine's Festival of Ballet: Scene-by-Scene Stories of 404 Classical & Contemporary Ballets.* New York: Doubleday, 1977; Comet, 1984, Vols. I & II. Vol. II includes three essays by Balanchine: "How to Enjoy Ballet," "A Brief History of the Ballet," and "How I Became a Dancer and Choreographer."

Cosi, Liliana. *The Young Ballet Dancer.* New York: Stein and Day, 1977. Many photographs of world-famous performers. Also clear pictures of students demonstrating ballet techniques at the Bolshoi Ballet School in Moscow and La Scala School in Milan. Written by a ballerina and teacher for young people.

Selected Bibliography

Franks, A.H., editor. *Pavlova, a Biography*. London: Burke, 1956. A biography on the twenty-fifth anniversary of Pavlova's death, edited by Franks in collaboration with members of the Pavlova Commemoration Committee.

Fonteyn, Margot. *Pavlova: Portrait of a Dancer*. Editors, John and Roberta Lazzarini. New York: Viking, 1984. Wonderful pictures and text by another extraordinary prima ballerina.

Gross, Ruth Belov. *If You Were a Ballet Dancer*. New York: Scholastic, 1979. In a question-and-answer format, this book describes for children what it is like to become a ballet dancer.

Kuklin, Susan. *Reaching for Dreams: A Ballet from Rehearsal to Opening Night*. New York: Lothrop, Lee & Shepard, 1987. Written for young adults and illustrated with photographs, this is an engaging chronicle of seven weeks in the life of the Alvin Ailey dance company as the dancers learn a new ballet.

Lazzarini, John and Roberta. *Pavlova: Repertoire of a Legend*. New York: Schirmer, 1980. A chronological history in text and pictures of Pavlova's career through her dance roles.

Malvern, Gladys. *Dancing Star: The Story of Anna Pavlova.* New York: Julian Messner, 1942. The only Pavlova biography specifically written for children.

Money, Keith. *Anna Pavlova: Her Life and Art.* New York: Alfred A. Knopf, 1982. Over four hundred pages of text and pictures, probably the most comprehensive biography of Pavlova yet published.

Montague, Sarah. *The Ballerina: Famous Dancers and Rising Stars of Our Time.* New York: Universe, 1980. After a brief history of the ballet, the collection of short biographies of twenty-six ballerinas and several new dancers begins with Anna Pavlova. Montague writes, "No dancer in history has been so much seen, described, and loved."

Morris, Ann. *On Their Toes: A Russian Ballet School.* New York: Antheneum, 1991. Illustrated with photographs, this children's book tells the story of student life today at the ballet school Pavlova attended one hundred years before.

Index